# franz schubert
1797-1828

a critical discography
of the piano music
compiled by john hunt

# Fremd bin ich eingezogen
## a critical discography of the piano music of Franz Schubert

### John Hunt

© John Hunt 2017

ISBN 978-1-901395-34-1

Travis & Emery Music Bookshop
17 Cecil Court
London
WC2N 4EZ
United Kingdom.
Tel. (+44) (0) 20 7240 2129.
newpublications@travis-and-emery.com

## Contents

**1/INTRODUCTION TO THE DISCOGRAPHY**/*page 7*

**2/FRANZ SCHUBERT: THE DEUTSCH CATALOGUE**/*page 13*

**3A/THE SONATAS: COMPLETE OR NEAR-COMPLETE SETS**/*page 59*

**3B/THE SONATAS: STANDARD COMPLETE SETS**/*page 63*

**3C/A SPECIAL CASE: SVIATOSLAV RICHTER**/*page 65*

**3D/LATE SONATAS**/*page 65*

**4/THE INDIVIDUAL SONATAS**/*page 66*

**5/FANTASY, IMPROMPTUS, MOMENTS MUSICAUX, KLAVIERSTUECKE AND OTHER SOLO PIECES**/*page 95*

*Contents/concluded*

**6/THE DANCE MUSIC FOR SOLO KEYBOARD: COMPLETE OR NEAR-COMPLETE SET**/*page 107*

**7/THE DANCE MUSIC FOR SOLO KEYBOARD: INDIVIDUAL SETS OF DANCES**/*page 109*

**8/THE KEYBOARD MUSIC FOR 4 HANDS**/*page 113*

**9/SVIATOSLAV RICHTER: THE SCHUBERT DISCOGRAPHY**/*page 125*

**10/ARTUR SCHNABEL: THE SCHUBERT DISCOGRAPHY**/*page 153*

**11/A REMARKABLE SCHUBERT EVENING**/*page 173*

**12/INDEX OF PIANISTS**/*page 177*

**13/POSTSCRIPT: SCHUBERT CDs FOR THE DESERT ISLAND**/*page 191*

## 1/INTRODUCTION TO THE DISCOGRAPHY

"Fremd bin ich eingezogen, fremd zieh' ich wieder aus"
- *I came here as a stranger, and as a stranger I'll depart*

Those opening words of the poet Wilhelm Müller for Schubert's song-cycle *Winterreise* seem to sum up a mood of loneliness which permeates Schubert's entire sound world, and nowhere more pointedly than in the works he composed for solo keyboard.

My first encounter with the piano music of Franz Schubert came in 1961, when Sviatoslav Richter, at one of his very first London recitals, played the final B Flat Sonata. I followed this up by listening to a Philips LP recording of the same sonata by the Rumanian pianist Clara Haskil – it was to be the start of a life-long obsession with the keyboard output of this quintessentially Viennese composer.

Fortunately I remained undeterred in my quest by the comments in *The Record Guide,* a music publication widely respected during the 1950s. On the subject of Schubert's *oeuvre* for solo piano, the guide had claimed that "his weaknesses as a composer are more evident in his piano music – especially the sonatas – than elsewhere in his work. Deeply unsophisticated, he took over, uncritically, the elaborate sonata form which had been evolved by his great predecessors,

*1/Introduction to the discography/continued*
and used it for the deployment of ideas that would not always stand the weight of so much expatiation. In some of the larger sonatas, full as they are of beautiful things, Schubert's longwindedness cannot always be felt as 'heavenly length'. Moreover his attitude to the instrument was as peculiar as Weber's, and much of his piano music is consequently very difficult indeed to bring off. The passage work is horribly tricky; nothing seems to lie under the hand....."

The writer of the above does go on to give credit for more accessible pieces like the Impromptus, but a charitable apology for this highly misleading over-all assessment must be to conclude that comparatively few recordings of the works in question were actually available at the time of writing those comments.

The B Flat Piano Sonata mentioned at the outset forms part of a group of masterpieces completed in the final months of the composer's short life – they also included two other sonatas as well as a clutch of works for piano duet, the String Quintet in C, *Lieder* which would eventually form the cycle known as *Schwanengesang* and the Great C Major Symphony. More significantly

*1/Introduction to the discography/continued*

for our purposes, this sonata constitutes the consummation of a corpus of music conceived for the keyboard of Schubert's time, a body of music which in my view is still undervalued both by musicologists and music lovers in general. It embraces not only sonatas (a form which had already been perfected by illustrious predecessors Haydn, Mozart and Beethoven) but also self-contained impromptus and *Klavierstücke,* fantasies (which would be a model for Schumann and Liszt), dances (in the form of *Deutsche Tänze, Walzer, Ländler, Ecossaises*) and a myriad of further dances and marches for piano duet (4 hands).

Schubert is quoted, perhaps a shade romantically, as having stated: "When I wanted to sing of love, it turned into pain; and when I wanted to sing only of pain, it turned into love". Yet this aphorism contains a strange resonance in the piano music (not to mention in the vast output of *Lieder*). Not for Schubert the lofty ideals and intellectual rigour of Beethoven, but rather a depiction of life in all its happiness alternating with sadness and depression (see the late sonatas and the *Winterreise* song cycle). Inspiration in the piano works can also often be heard to derive from themes already used in the *Lieder*, where the disciplne of brevity imbues them with poignant directness.

*1/Introduction to the discography/continued*

My aim in the discography is to guide the listener's journey by pointing out, or recommending, key versions in the music's recorded history. There can be no claim to comprehensiveness, rather a personal selection. I start with a section on the complete (or near complete) recordings of the sonatas, then go on to examining records of the individual sonatas: regarding these, I would recommend the detailed commentary provided by Paul Badura-Skoda for his latest survey of the sonatas – it is available, not with the boxed set of CDs, but on the website www.outhere-music.com.

After the Sonatas, there follows similar treatment for the Impromptus, *Klavierstücke* and Dances, and finally the considerable body of music written by Schubert for piano duet for performance in the intimate circle of his friends and colleagues. Before all this, however, I begin by listing all of Schubert's *oeuvre* so that the piano music is placed in context. Numbering of the works is that of the now fully accepted Otto Erich Deutsch, only published as recently as 1951 but with some later amendments (I have used the edition issued by Bärenreiter as *Der kleine Deutsch* in 1983).

*1/Introduction to the discography/concluded*

For ease of reference I have added the complete Schubert discographies of two of the indisputably most important interpreters (Artur Schnabel and Sviatoslav Richter): these are updated from the listings previously published in my discographies *Giants of the Keyboard* (1994) and *Pianist of the Century* (1999) respectively.

A final section in the book reproduces my concert review, originally written for the periodical *Musical Opinion*, of a remarkable Schubert recital at London's Wigmore Hall by Christian Blackshaw.

I must also gratefully acknowledge help and stimulation in preparing the discography from friends and colleagues Edward Allnatt, John Baker, Martin Bligh, Olivier Brunel, Philip Chang, John Hancock, Roderick Krüsemann, David Patmore and Graham Silcock.

John Hunt  2017

## 2/FRANZ SCHUBERT: THE DEUTSCH CATALOGUE

*The piano works appear in bold type*

**001     Fantasy in G for 4 hands/April-May 1810**
001a    Song accompaniment in C/1810/incomplete
**001b   Fantasy in G for 4 hands/1810-1811/incomplete**
**001c   Sonata in F for 4 hands/1810-1811/incomplete**
002     Movement in G for string quartet/incomplete
002a    Overture in D/1811/incomplete
002b    Symphony in D/1811/incomplete
002c    Movement in D or F for string quartet/1811/incomplete
**002d   6 Minuets/1811**
**002e   Fantasy in C/1811**
002f    Trio in C for a minuet/1811
003     Movement in C for string quartet/1812/incomplete
004     Overture to *Der Teufel als Hydraulicus*/1812
005     Lied: *Hagars Klage*/March 1811
006     Lied: *Des Mädchens Klage*/1811-1812
007     Lied: *Leichenfantasie*/1811
008     Overture in C for string quintet/June 1811
008a    Overture in C for string quartet/July 1811
**009     Fantasy in G for 4 hands/September 1811**
010     Lied: *Der Vatermörder*/December 1811
011     Singspiel: *Der Spiegelritter*/December 1811/incomplete
012     Overture in D/1811-1812
**013     Fugue in D/1812**
**014     Piano sketch for an overture/1812**
015     Lied: *Der Geistertanz*/2 versions/1812

2/*Deutsch Catalogue/continued*

| | | |
|---|---|---|
| 016 | 7 Contrapunctal exercises/undated | |
| 017 | 9 Vocal exercises on Metastasio's *Isacco*/1812 | |
| 018 | String Quartet in G/1810-1811 | |
| 019 | String Quartet/1810-1811/lost | |
| 019a | String Quartet/1810-1811/lost | |
| **019b** | **Waltzes and March/1812-1813/lost** | |
| 020 | Overture in B for string quartet/1812/lost | |
| **021** | **6 Variations in E flat/1812/lost** | |
| **022** | **12 Minuets with Trios/1812/lost** | |
| 023 | Lied: *Klagelied*/1812 | |
| **024** | **7 Variations in F/1812/incomplete** | |
| **024a** | **Fugue in C/1812** | |
| **024b** | **Fugue in G/1812** | |
| **024c** | **Fugue in D/1813** | |
| **024d** | **Fugue in C/1812/incomplete** | |
| 024e | Mass in F/1812/incomplete | |
| 025 | Contrapunctal exercises/June 1812 | |
| 025b | Contrapunctal exercises/1812 | |
| 025c | Fugue in F for 2 voices/1812 | |
| 026 | Overture in D/June 1812 | |
| 027 | Salve regina in F/June 1812 | |
| 028 | Trio in B for piano, violin and cello/July-August 1812 | |
| **029** | **Andante in C/September 1812** | |

*2/Deutsch catalogue/continued*

030  Lied: *Der Jüngling am Bache*/first version/September 1812
031  Kyrie in D/September 1812
032  String Quartet in C/September-October 1812
033  6 Compositional Studies on Metastasio's *Isacco*/1812
034  Vocal Quartet in D on *Te solo adoro*/November 1812
035  3 Compositional Studies on *Serbate o dei custodi*/1812
036  String Quartet in B/November 1812-February 1813
037  Vocal Trio: *Die Advokaten*/December 1812
**037a  4 Sketches for Fugues/1813**
038  Vocal Trio: *Totengräberlied*/1813
039  Lied: *Lebenstraum*/1810/incomplete
039a  3 Orchestral minuets and trios/1813/lost
040  String Quartet in E flat/lost
**041  30 Minuets and trios/1813/partially lost**
**041a  Fugue in E/1813/incomplete**
042  Aria: *Misero pargoletto*/1813/2 versions
043  Vocal Trio: *Dreifach ist der Schritt der Zeit*/July 1813
044  Lied: *Totengräberlied*/January 1813
045  Kyrie in B/March 1813
046  String Quartet in C/March 1813
047  Dithyrambe: *Nimmer erscheinen die Götter*/March 1813
**048  Fantasy in C for 4 hands/April-June 1813**

*2/Deutsch catalogue/continued*

049 Kyrie in D/April 1813
050 Lied: *Die Schatten*/April 1813
051 Vocal Trio: *Unendliche Freude*/April 1813/first version
052 Lied: *Sehnsucht*/April 1813
053 Vocal Trio: *Vorüber die stöhnende Klage*/April 1813
054 Vocal Trio: *Unendliche Freude*/April 1813/second version
055 Vocal Trio: *Selig durch die Liebe*/April 1813
056 Canon for 3 voices: *Sanctus*/April 1813
057 Vocal Trio: *Hier strecket der wallende Pilger*/April 1813
058 Vocal Trio: *Dessen Fahne Donnerstürme wallte*/May 1813
059 Lied: *Verklärung*/May 1813
060 Vocal Trio: *Hier umarmen sich getreue Gatten*/October 1813
061 Canon for 3 voices: *Ein jugendlicher Maienschwung*/May 1813
062 Vocal Trio: *Thronend auf erhabnem Sitz*/May 1813
063 Vocal Trio: *Wer die steile Sternenbahn*/May 1813
064 Vocal Trio: *Majestätische Sonnenrose*/May 1813
065 Canon for 3 voices: *Schmerz verzerret ihr Gesicht*/May 1813
066 Kyrie in F/May 1813
067 Vocal Trio: *Frisch atmet des Morgens lebendiger Hauch*/1813
068 String Quartet in B/June-August 1813/incomplete
069 Canon for 3 voices: *Dreifach ist der Schritt der Zeit*/July 1813
070 Vocal Trio: *Dreifach ist der Schritt der Zeit*/July 1813
071 Vocal Trio: *Die zwei Tugendwege*/July 1813
071a Canon for 3 voices: *Alleluja*/July 1813
**071b Fugue in E/July 1813**
071c Orchesterstück in D/August-September 1813/incomplete

*2/Deutsch catalogue/continued*

072    Octet in F for wind/August 1813/incomplete
073    Lied: *Thekla*/August 1813
074    String Quartet in D/August-September 1813
075    Lied: *Trinklied*/August 1813
076    Aria: *Pensa che questo istante*/September 1813
077    *Lied*: *Der Taucher*/September 1813/first version
078    Aria: *Son fra l'onde*/September 1813
079    Nonet for wind in E flat/September 1813
080    Vocal Trio: *Zur Namensfeier meines Vaters*/September 1813
081    Lied: *Auf den Sieg der Deutschen*/1813
082    Symphony No 1 in D/October 1813
083    Lied: *Zur Namensfeier des Herrn Andreas Siller*/1813
084    Singspiel: *Des Teufels Lustschloss*/October 1813-May 1814
085    Offertorium in C/incomplete
086    Minuet in D for string quartet/November 1813
087    String Quartet in E flat/November 1813
087a  Andante in C for string quartet/November 1813/incomplete
088    Canon for 3 voices: *Verschwunden sind die Schmerzen*/1813
089    5 Minuets & 6 Trios for string quartet/November 1813
090    5 Deutsche Tänze & 7 trios for string quartet/November 1813
**091    2 Minuets and 2 trios/November 1813**
092    Canon for 2 voices after Mozart: *Lass immer in der Jugendglanz*
093    Liederzyklus: *Don Gayseros*/1815
094    String Quartet in D/1811-1812
094a  Orchesterstück in B/1814/incomplete
094b  5 Minuets & 6 Tänze for string quartet & horns/1814/lost
095    Lied: *Adelaide*/1814

*2/Deutsch catalogue/continued*

| | | |
|---|---|---|
| 096 | Quartet in G for flute, viola, guitar and cello | |
| 097 | Lied: *An Elisa*/1814 | |
| 098 | Lied: *Erinnerungen*/1814/first version/incomplete | |
| 099 | Lied: *Andenken*/April 1814/first version | |
| 100 | Lied: *Geisternähe*/April 1814 | |
| 101 | Lied: *Erinnerung*/April 1814 | |
| 102 | Lied: *Die Betende*/1814 | |
| 103 | String quartet movement in C/April 1814/partially lost | |
| 104 | Lied: *Die Befreier Europas in Paris*/May 1814 | |
| 105 | Mass in F/May-June 1814 | |
| 106 | Salve regina in B/June-July 1814 | |
| 107 | Lied: *Lied aus der Ferne*/July 1814/2 versions | |
| 108 | Lied: *Der Abend*/July 1814 | |
| 109 | Lied: *Lied der Liebe*/July 1814 | |
| 110 | Aria for bass and chorus: *Wer ist gross?*/1814/partially lost | |
| 111 | Lied: *Der Taucher*/second version | |
| 112 | String Quartet in B/September 1814 | |
| 113 | Lied: *An Emma*/September 1814/three versions | |
| 114 | Lied: *Romanze*/September 1814/two versions | |
| 115 | Lied: *An Laura*/October 1814 | |
| 116 | Lied: *Der Geistertanz*/October 1814/third version | |
| 117 | Lied: *Das Mädchen aus der Fremde*/October 1814 | |
| 118 | Lied: *Gretchen am Spinnrade*/October 1814 | |
| 119 | Lied: *Nachtgesang*/November 1814 | |
| 120 | Lied: *Trost in Tränen*/November 1814 | |

*2/Deutsch catalogue/continued*

| | | |
|---|---|---|
| 121 | Lied: *Schäfers Klagelied*/November 1814/2 versions |
| 122 | Lied: *Ammenlied*/December 1814 |
| 123 | Lied: *Sehnsucht*/December 1814 |
| 124 | Lied: *Am See*/December 1814/2 versions |
| 125 | Symphony No 2 in B/December 1814-March 1815 |
| 126 | Lied (Duet): *Szene aus Faust*/December 1814/2 versions |
| 127 | Canon for 2 voices after Mozart: *Selig sind die im Herrn* |
| **128** | **12 Wiener Deutsche Tänze/1812** |
| 129 | Trio: *Mailied*/1815/first version |
| 130 | Canon for 3 voices: *Der Schnee zerrinnt*/1815/first version |
| 131 | Canon for 3 voices: *Lacrimoso son io*/August 1815/2 versions |
| 132 | Trio (Quartet): *Lied beim Rundetanz* |
| 133 | Trio (Quartet): *Lied im Freien* |
| 134 | Lied: *Ballade*/1815 |
| **135** | **Deutscher Tanz with Trio in E/1815** |
| 136 | Offertorium in C/1815 |
| 137 | Singspiel: *Adrest*/1817-1819/incomplete |
| 138 | Lied: *Rastlose Liebe*/May 1815/2 versions |
| **139** | **Deutscher Tanz in C sharp with Trio in A/1815** |

*2/Deutsch catalogue/continued*

140  Trio: *Klage um Ali Bey*/1815
141  Lied: *Der Mondabend*/1815
142  Lied: *Geistesgruss*/March 1816/6 versions
143  Lied: *Genugsamkeit*/1815
144  Lied: *Romanze*/April 1816
**145  12 Waltzes, 17 Ländler and 9 Ecossaises/1815-1821**
**146  20 Waltzes/1815-1823**
147  Trio: *Bardengesang*/January 1816
148  Aria for tenor and chorus: *Trinklied*/February 1815
149  Lied: *Der Sänger*/February 1815/2 versions
150  Lied: *Lodas Gespenst*/January 1816
151  Lied: *Auf einen Kirchhof*/February 1815
152  Lied: *Minona*/February 1815
153  Lied: *Als ich sie erröten sah*/February 1815
**154  Sonata in E/February 1815/incomplete**
155  Lied: *Das Bild*/February 1815
**156  10 Variations in F/February 1815**
**157  Sonata in E/February 1815**
**158  Ecossaise in D minor/February 1815**
159  Lied: *Die Erwartung*/May 1816/2 versions
160  Lied: *Am Flusse*/February 1815/first version
161  Lied: *An Mignon*/February 1815/2 versions
162  Lied: *Nähe des Geliebten*/February 1815/2 versions
163  Lied: *Sängers Morgenlied*/February 1815/first version

*2/Deutsch catalogue/continued*

| | | |
|---|---|---|
| 164 | Lied: | *Liebesrausch*/March 1815/first version/incomplete |
| 165 | Lied: | *Sängers Morgenlied*/March 1815/second version |
| 166 | Lied: | *Amphiaraos*/March 1815 |
| 167 | Mass in G/March 1815 | |
| 168 | Chorlied: | *Nun lasst uns den Leib begraben*/March 1815 |
| 168a | Chorlied: | *Jesus Christus unser Heiland*/March 1815 |
| 169 | Chorlied: | *Trinklied vor der Schlacht*/March 1815 |
| 170 | Chorlied: | *Schwertlied*/March 1815 |
| 171 | Lied: | *Gebet vor der Schlacht*/March 1815 |
| 172 | Lied: | *Der Morgenstern*/March 1815 |
| 173 | String Quartet in G/March-April 1815 | |
| 174 | Lied: | *Das war ich*/March 1815 |
| 175 | Stabat mater in G/April 1815 | |
| 176 | Lied: | *Die Sterne*/April 1815 |
| 177 | Lied: | *Vergebliche Liebe*/April 1815 |
| **178** | **Adagio in G/April 1815/2 versions** | |
| 179 | Lied: | *Liebesrausch*/April 1815/second version |
| 180 | Lied: | *Sehnsucht der Liebe*/April 1815 |
| 181 | Offertorium in A/April 1815 | |
| 182 | Lied: | *Die erste Liebe*/April 1815 |
| 183 | Chorlied: | *Trinklied*/April 1815 |
| 184 | Graduale in C/April 1815 | |

*2/Deutsch catalogue/continued*

| | | |
|---|---|---|
| 185 | Dona nobis pacem for Mass in F/second version | |
| 186 | Lied: *Die Sterbende*/May 1815 | |
| 187 | Lied: *Stimme der Liebe*/May 1815/first version | |
| 188 | Lied: *Naturgenuss*/May 1815/first version | |
| 189 | Chorlied: *An die Freude*/May 1815 | |
| 190 | Singspiel: *Der vierjährige Posten*/May 1815 | |
| 191 | Lied: *Des Mädchens Klage*/May 1815/2 versions | |
| 192 | Lied: *Der Jüngling am Bache*/May 1815/second version | |
| 193 | Lied: *An den Mond*/May 1815/2 versions | |
| 194 | Lied: *Die Mainacht*/May 1815 | |
| 195 | Lied: *Amalia*/May 1815 | |
| 196 | Lied: *An die Nachtigall*/May 1815 | |
| 197 | Lied: *An die Apfelbäume*/May 1815 | |
| 198 | Lied: *Seufzer*/May 1815 | |
| 199 | Duet for voices or horns: *Mailied*/May 1815/second version | |
| 200 | Symphony No 3 in D/May-July 1815 | |
| 201 | Lied: *Auf den Tod einer Nachtigall*/May 1815/first version | |
| 202 | Duet for voices or horns: *Der Schnee zerrinnt*/second version | |
| 203 | Duet for voices or horns: *Der Morgenstern*/second version | |
| 204 | Duet for voices or horns: *Jägerlied*/May 1815 | |
| 204a | Lied: *Das Traumbild*/May 1815/lost | |
| 205 | Duet for voices or horns: *Lützows wilde Jagd*/May 1815 | |
| 206 | Lied: *Liebeständelei*/May 1815 | |
| 207 | Lied: *Der Liebende*/May 1815 | |
| 208 | Lied: *Die Nonne*/May 1815/2 versions | |
| 209 | Lied: *Der Liedler*/January 1815 | |

*2/Deutsch catalogue/continued*

| | | |
|---|---|---|
| 210 | Lied: | *Die Liebe (Klärchens Lied)*/June 1815 |
| 211 | Lied: | *Adelheid und Emma*/June 1815 |
| 212 | Lied: | *Die Nonne*/second version |
| 213 | Lied: | *Der Traum*/June 1815 |
| 214 | Lied: | *Die Laube*/June 1815 |
| 215 | Lied: | *Jägers Abendlied*/June 1815/first version |
| 215a | Lied: | *Meeresstille*/June 1815/first version |
| 216 | Lied: | *Meeresstille*/June 1815/second version |
| 217 | Lied: | *Kolmas Klage*/June 1815 |
| 218 | Lied: | *Grablied*/June 1815 |
| 219 | Lied: | *Das Finden*/June 1815 |
| 220 | Singspiel: | *Fernando*/July 1815 |
| 221 | Lied: | *Der Abend*/July 1815 |
| 222 | Lied: | *Lieb Minna*/July 1815 |
| 223 | Salve regina in F/July 1815/first version | |
| 224 | Lied: | *Wandrers Nachtlied*/July 1815 |
| 225 | Lied: | *Der Fischer*/July 1815/2 versions |
| 226 | Lied: | *Erster Verlust*/July 1815 |
| 227 | Lied: | *Idens Nachtgesang*/July 1815 |
| 228 | Lied: | *Von Ida*/July 1815 |
| 229 | Lied: | *Die Erscheinung*/July 1815 |
| 230 | Lied: | *Die Täuschung*/July 1815 |
| 231 | Lied: | *Das Sehnen*/July 1815 |

*2/Deutsch catalogue/continued*

| | | |
|---|---|---|
| 232 | Vocal Quartet: | *Hymne an die Unendlichen*/July 1815 |
| 233 | Lied: | *Geist der Liebe*/July 1815 |
| 234 | Lied: | *Tischlied*/July 1815 |
| 235 | Lied: | *Abends unter der Linde*/July 1815/first version |
| 236 | Vocal Trio: | *Das Abendbrot*/July 1815 |
| 237 | Lied: | *Abends unter der Liebe*/July 1815/second version |
| 238 | Lied: | *Die Mondnacht*/July 1815 |
| 239 | Singspiel: | *Claudine von Villa Bella*/July 1815 |
| 240 | Lied: | *Huldigung*/July 1815 |
| 241 | Lied: | *Alles um Liebe*/July 1815 |
| 242 | Vocal Trio: | *Trinklied im Winter*/August 1815 |
| 243 | Vocal Trio: | *Frühlingslied*/August 1815/first version |
| 244 | Canon for 3 voices: | *Willkommen lieber schöner Mai*/August 1815 |
| 245 | Lied: | *An den Frühling*/third version |
| 246 | Lied: | *Die Bürgschaft*/August 1815 |
| 247 | Lied: | *Die Spinnerin*/August 1815 |
| 248 | Lied: | *Lob des Tokayers*/August 1815 |
| 249 | March accompaniment: | *Die Schlacht*/August 1815 |
| 250 | Lied: | *Das Geheimnis*/August 1815/first version |
| 251 | Lied: | *Hoffnung*/August 1815/first version |
| 252 | Lied: | *Das Mädchen aus der Fremde*/August 1815/second version |
| 253 | Lied/Duet: | *Punschlied*/August 1815/2 versions |
| 254 | Lied: | *Der Gott und die Bajadere*/August 1815 |
| 255 | Lied: | *Der Rattenfänger*/August 1815 |

*2/Deutsch catalogue/continued*

| | | |
|---|---|---|
| 256 | Lied: | *Der Schatzgräber*/August 1815 |
| 257 | Lied: | *Heidenröslein*/August 1815 |
| 258 | Lied: | *Bundeslied*/August 1815 |
| 259 | Lied: | *An den Mond*/August 1815/first version |
| 260 | Lied: | *Wonne der Wehmut*/August 1815 |
| 261 | Lied: | *Wer kauft Liebesgötter?*/August 1815 |
| 262 | Lied: | *Die Fröhlichkeit*/August 1815 |
| 263 | Lied: | *Cora an die Sonne*/August 1815 |
| 264 | Lied: | *Der Morgenkuss*/August 1815/2 versions |
| 265 | Lied: | *Abendständchen an Lina*/August 1815 |
| 266 | Lied: | *Morgenlied*/August 1815 |
| 267 | Vocal Quartet: | *Trinklied*/August 1815 |
| 268 | Vocal Quartet: | *Bergknappenlied*/August 1815 |
| 269 | Vocal Trio: | *Das Leben*/August 1815/2 versions |
| 270 | Lied: | *An die Sonne (Sinke liebe Sonne!)*/August 1815 |
| 271 | Lied: | *Der Weiberfreund*/August 1815 |
| 272 | Lied: | *An die Sonne (Königliche Morgensonne)*/August 1815 |
| 273 | Lied: | *Lilla an die Morgenröte*/August 1815 |
| 274 | Lied: | *Tischlerlied*/August 1815 |
| 275 | Lied: | *Totenkranz für ein Kind*/August 1815 |
| 276 | Lied: | *Abendlied*/August 1815 |
| 277 | Vocal Trio: | *Punschlied*/August 1815 |
| **277a** | **Minuet in A with Trio in F/September 1815** | |

*2/Deutsch catalogue/continued*

278  Lied: *Ossians Lied nach dem Falle Nathos*/1815/2 versions
**279  Sonata in C/September 1815**
280  Lied: *Das Rosenband*/September 1815
281  Lied: *Das Mädchen von Inistore*/September 1815
282  Lied: *Cronnan*/September 1815
283  Lied: *An den Frühling*/September 1815/first version
284  Lied: *Es ist so angenehm*/September 1815
285  Lied: *Furcht der* Geliebten/An *Cidli*/September 1815/2 versions
286  Lied: *Selma und Selmar*/September 1815/2 versions
287  Lied: *Vaterlandslied*/September 1815/2 versions
288  Lied: *An Sie*/September 1815
289  Lied: *Die Sommernacht*/September 1815/2 versions
290  Lied: *Die frühen Gräber*/September 1815
291  Lied: *Dem Unendlichen*/September 1815/3 versions
292  Lied: *Klage*/sketch for a later version
293  Lied: *Shilric und Vinvela*/September 1815
294  Gratulations-Kantate (Namensfeier)/September 1815
295  Lied: *Hoffnung*/1815-1816/2 versions
296  Lied: *An den Mond*/1815-1816/second version
297  Lied: *Augenlied*/1817/2 versions
298  Lied: *Liane*/October 1815
**299  12 Ecossaises/October 1815**
300  Lied: *Der Jüngling an der Quelle*/1816-1817
301  Lied: *Lambertine*/October 1815
302  Lied: *Labetrank der Liebe*/October 1815

*2/Deutsch catalogue/continued*

| | | |
|---|---|---|
| 303 | Lied: | *An die Geliebte*/October 1815 |
| 304 | Lied: | *Wiegenlied*/October 1815 |
| 305 | Lied: | *Mein Gruss an den Mai*/October 1815 |
| 306 | Lied: | *Skolie*/October 1815 |
| 307 | Lied: | *Die Sternenwelten*/October 1815 |
| 308 | Lied: | *Die Macht der Liebe*/October 1815 |
| 309 | Lied: | *Das gestörte Glück*/October 1815 |
| 310 | Lied: | *Nur wer die Sehnsucht kennt*/October 1815/first version |
| 311 | Lied: | *An den Mond*/October 1815/sketch without text |
| 312 | Lied: | *Hektors Abschied*/October 1815/2 versions |
| 313 | Lied: | *Die Sterne*/October 1815 |
| 314 | Lied: | *Nachtgesang*/October 1815 |
| 315 | Lied: | *An Rosa 1*/October 1815 |
| 316 | Lied: | *An Rosa 2*/October 1815/2 versions |
| 317 | Lied: | *Idens Schwanenlied*/October 1815/2 versions |
| 318 | Lied: | *Schwanengesang*/October 1815 |
| 319 | Lied: | *Luisens Antwort*/October 1815 |
| 320 | Lied: | *Der Zufriedene*/October 1815 |
| 321 | Lied: | *Mignon (Kennst du das Land?)*/October 1815 |
| 322 | Lied: | *Hermann und Thusnelda*/October 1815 |
| 323 | Lied: | *Klage der Ceres*/November 1815-June 1816 |
| 324 | Mass in B/November 1815 | |
| 325 | Lied: | *Wer sich der Einsamkeit ergibt*/November 1815/first version |
| 326 | Singspiel: | *Die Freunde von Salamanca*/November-December 1815 |
| 327 | Lied: | *Lorma*/November 1815/first version |

## 2/Deutsch catalogue/continued

328  Lied: *Erlkönig*/October 1815/4 versions
329  Lied: *Die drei Sänger*/December 1815/incomplete
329a Canon: *Das Grab*/December 1815/sketch for first version
330  Chorlied: *Das Grab*/December 1815/second version
331  Vocal Quartet: *Die Entfernten*/1816/first version
332  Vocal Trio: *Die Entfernten*/1816/second version
333  Vocal Trio: *Lass dein Vertrauen nicht schwinden*
**334  Minuet in A with Trio in E/1815**
**335  Minuet with 2 Trios in E/1813**
**336  Minuet with Trio in D/dubious**
337  Vocal Quartet: *Die Einsiedelei*/1816/first version
338  Vocal Quartet: *An den Frühling*/1816/second version
339  Vocal Trio/Quartet: *Amors Macht*
340  Vocal Trio/Quartet: *Badelied*
341  Vocal Trio/Quartet: *Sylphen*
342  Lied: *An mein Klavier*/1816
343  Lied: *Litanei auf das Fest Allerseelen*/1816/2 versions
344  Lied: *Am ersten Maimorgen*/1816
345  Konzertstück in D for violin and orchestra/1816
**346  Allegretto in C/1816/incomplete**
**347  Allegro moderato in C/1813/incomplete**
**348  Andantino in C/1816/incomplete**
**349  Adagio in C/1816/incomplete**
350  Lied: *Der Entfernten*/1816/second version

*2/Deutsch catalogue/continued*

351  Lied: *Fischerlied*/1816/first version
352  Vocal Duet: *Licht und Liebe*/1816
353  String Quartet in E/1816
**354  4 Komische Ländler/January 1816**
355  8 Ländler for violin in F sharp/January 1816
356  Chorlied: *Trinklied*/1816/incomplete
357  Canon: *Goldner Schein*/May 1816
358  Lied: *Die Nacht*
359  Lied: *Nur wer die Sehnsucht kennt*/1816/second version
360  Lied: *Lied eines Schiffers an die Dioskuren*/1816
361  Lied: *Am Bach im Frühling*/1816/2 versions
362  Lied: *Zufriedenheit*/1815-1816/first version
363  Lied: *An Chloen*/1816/incomplete
364  Vocal Quartet: *Fischerlied*/1816-1817/second version
**365  36 Originaltänze/1818-1821**
**366  17 Ländler/July-November 1824**
367  Lied: *Der König in Thule*/1816
368  Lied: *Jägers Abendlied*/1816/second version
369  Lied: *An Schwager Kronos*/1816
370  9 Ländler for violin in D/January 1816
371  Lied: *Klage*/January 1816
372  Lied: *An die Natur*/January 1816
373  Lied: *Mutter geht durch ihre Kammern*/January 1816
374  11 Ländler for violin in B/February 1816
375  Lied: *Der Tod Oskars*/February 1816

*2/Deutsch catalogue/continued*

376  Lied: *Lorma*/February 1816/second version
377  Chorlied: *Das Grab*/February 1816/third version
**378  8 Ländler in B/February 1816**
379  Deutsches Salve regina in F/February 1816
**380  3 Minuets each with 2 Trios/February 1816/incomplete**
381  Lied: *Morgenlied*/February 1816
382  Lied: *Abendlied*/February 1816
383  Stabat mater/February 1816
384  Violin Sonata in D/March 1816
385  Violin Sonata in A/March 1816
386  Salve regina in B/1816
387  Cantata: *Die Schlacht*/March 1816/sketch for a second version
388  Lied: *Laura am Klavier*/March 1816/2 versions
389  Lied: *Des Mädchens Klage*/March 1816/third version
390  Lied: *Entzückung an Laura*/March 1816/first version
391  Lied: *Die vier Weltalter*/March 1816
392  Lied: *Pflügerlied*/March 1816
393  Lied: *Die Einsiedelei*/March 1816/second version
394  Lied: *An die Harmonie*/March 1816
395  Lied: *Lebensmelodien*/March 1816
396  Lied: *Gruppe aus dem Tartarus*/March 1816/first version
397  Lied: *Ritter Toggenburg*/March 1816
398  Lied: *Frühlingslied*/May 1816/second version
399  Lied: *Auf den Tod einer Nachtigall*/May 1816/second version

*2/Deutsch catalogue/continued*

400 Lied: *Die Knabenzeit*/May 1816
401 Lied: *Winterlied*/May 1816
402 Lied: *Der Flüchtling*/March 1816
403 Lied: *Ins stille Land*/March 1816/4 versions
404 Lied: *Die Herbstnacht*/March 1816
405 Lied: *Der Herbstabend*/April 1816/2 versions
406 Lied: *Abschied von der Harfe*/March 1816
407 Beitrag zur 50-jährigen Jubelfeier von Salieri/June 1816
408 Violin Sonata in G/April 1816
409 Lied: *Die verfehlte Stunde*/April 1816
410 Lied: *Sprache der Liebe*/April 1816
411 Lied: *Daphne am Bach*/April 1816
412 Lied: *Stimme der Liebe*/April 1816/2 versions
413 Lied: *Entzückung*/April 1816
414 Lied: *Geist der Liebe*/April 1816/first version
415 Lied: *Klage*/April 1816
416 Lied: *Lied in der Abwesenheit*/April 1816/incomplete
417 Symphony in C "Tragic"/April 1816
418 Lied: *Stimme der Liebe*/April 1816/second version
419 Lied: *Julius am Theone*/April 1816
**420** **12 Deutsche Tänze/1816**
**421** **6 Ecossaises/1816**
422 Vocal Quartet: *Naturgemäss*/1822
423 Vocal Trio: *Andenken*/May 1816
424 Vocal Trio: *Erinnerungen*/May 1816/second version

*2/Deutsch catalogue/continued*

425  Vocal Trio: *Lebensbild*/May 1816/lost
426  Vocal Trio: *Trinklied*/May 1816/lost
427  Vocal Trio: *Trinklied im Mai*/May 1816
428  Vocal Trio: *Widerhall*/May 1816
429  Lied: *Minnelied*/May 1816
430  Lied: *Die frühe Liebe*/May 1816/2 versions
431  Lied: *Blumenlied*/May 1816
432  Lied: *Der Leidende*/May 1816/2 versions
433  Lied: *Seligkeit*/May 1816
434  Lied: *Erntelied*/May 1816
435  Opera: *Die Bürgschaft*/May 1816/incomplete
436  Lied: *Klage*/May 1816/first version
437  Lied: *Klage*/May 1816/second version
438  Rondo in A for violin and strings/June 1816
439  Vocal Quartet: *An die Sonne*/June 1816
440  Chorlied: *Chor der Engel*/June 1816
441  Vocal Trio: *Gütigster Bester Weisester!*
442  Chorlied: *Das grosse Halleluja*/June 1816
443  Chorlied: *Schlachtlied*/June 1816
444  Lied: *Die Gestirne*/June 1816
445  Lied: *Edone*/June 1816
446  Lied: *Die Liebesgötter*/June 1816
447  Lied: *An den Schlaf*/June 1816
448  Lied: *Gott im Frühlinge*/June 1816/2 versions
449  Lied: *Der gute Hirt*/June 1816

*2/Deutsch catalogue/continued*

| | | |
|---|---|---|
| 450 | Lied: *Fragment aus dem Aeschylus*/June 1816/2 versions |
| 451 | Cantata: *Prometheus*/June 1816/lost |
| 452 | Mass in C/June-July 1816 |
| 453 | Requiem in C/July 1816/incomplete |
| 454 | Lied: *Grablied auf einen Soldaten*/July 1816 |
| 455 | Lied: *Freude der Kinderjahre*/July 1816 |
| 456 | Lied: *Das Heimweh*/July 1816 |
| 457 | Lied: *An die untergehende Sonne*/May 1817 |
| 458 | Lied: *Aus Diego Manazares*/July 1816 |
| **459** | **Sonata in E/August 1816** |
| **459a** | **3 Klavierstücke/1816** |
| 460 | Tantum ergo in C/August 1816 |
| 461 | Tantum ergo in C/August 1816 |
| 462 | Lied: *An Chloen*/August 1816 |
| 463 | Lied: *Hochzeitlied*/August 1816 |
| 464 | Lied: *In der Mitternacht*/August 1816 |
| 465 | Lied: *Trauer der Liebe*/August 1816/2 versions |
| 466 | Lied: *Die Perle*/August 1816 |
| 467 | Lied: *Pflicht und Liebe*/August 1816/incomplete |
| 468 | Lied: *An den Mond*/August 1816 |
| 469 | Lied: *So lasst mich scheinen*/September 1816/first version |
| 470 | Overture in B/September 1816 |
| 471 | String Trio in B/September 1816/incomplete |
| 472 | Kantate zu Ehren von Josef Spendou/September 1816 |
| 473 | Lied: *Liedesend*/September 1816/2 versions |
| 474 | Lied: *Lied des Orpheus*/September 1816/2 versions |

*2/Deutsch catalogue/continued*

| | | |
|---|---|---|
| 475 | Lied: | *Abschied*/September 1816 |
| 476 | Lied: | *Rückweg*/September 1816 |
| 477 | Lied: | *Alte Liebe rostet nie*/September 1816 |
| 478 | Lieder: | *Gesänge des Harfners*/1816-1822/2 versions |
| 479 | Lied: | *An die Türen will ich schleichen* |
| 480 | Lied: | *Wer nie sein Brot mit Tränen ass* |
| 481 | Lied: | *Nur wer die Sehnsucht kennt*/September 1816/third version |
| 482 | Lied: | *Der Sänger am Felsen*/September 1816 |
| 483 | Lied: | *Ferne von der grossen Stadt*/September 1816 |
| 484 | Lied: | *Gesang der Geister über den Wassern*/1816/incomplete |
| 485 | | Symphony in B Flat/September-October 1816 |
| 486 | | Magnificat in C/September 1816 |
| 487 | | Adagio & Rondo concertante for Piano quartet/October 1816 |
| 488 | Duet: | *Auguste jam coelestium*/October 1816 |
| 489 | Lied: | *Der Wanderer*/October 1816/first version |
| 490 | Lied: | *Der Hirt*/October 1816 |
| 491 | Lied: | *Geheimnis*/October 1816 |
| 492 | Lied: | *Zum Punsche*/October 1816 |
| 493 | Lied: | *Der Wanderer*/second and third versions |
| 494 | Vocal Quintet: | *Der Geistertanz*/November 1816/fourth version |
| 495 | Lied: | *Abschied der Fürstin*/November 1816 |
| 496 | Lied: | *Bei dem Grabe meines Vaters*/November 1816 |
| 496a | Lied: | *Klage um Ali Bey*/November 1816 |
| 497 | Lied: | *An die Nachtigall*/November 1816 |
| 498 | Lied: | *Wiegenlied*/November 1816 |
| 499 | Lied: | *Abendlied*/November 1816 |

*2/Deutsch catalogue/continued*

| | | |
|---|---|---|
| 500 | Lied: | *Phidile*/November 1816 |
| 501 | Lied: | *Zufriedenheit*/November 1816/second version |
| 502 | Lied: | *Herbstlied*/November 1816 |
| 503 | Lied: | *Mailied*/November 1816/third version |
| 504 | Lied: | *Am Grabe Anselmos*/November 1816/2 versions |
| **505** | | **Adagio in D flat/September 1818** |
| **506** | | **Rondo in E/June 1817** |
| 507 | Lied: | *Skolie*/December 1816 |
| 508 | Lied: | *Lebenslied*/December 1816 |
| 509 | Lied: | *Leiden der Trennung*/December 1816/2 versions |
| 510 | Aria: | *Vedi quanto adoro*/December 1816 |
| **511** | | **Ecossaise in E flat/1817** |
| 512 | Lied: | *Klage (Nimmer länger trag' ich)*/dubious |
| 513 | Vocal Quartet: | *La pastorella al prato*/1817/first version |
| 513a | Lied: | *Nur wer die Liebe kennt*/1817/sketch |
| 514 | Lied: | *Die abgeblühte Linde*/1817 |
| 515 | Lied: | *Der Flug der Zeit*/1817 |
| 516 | Lied: | *Sehnsucht*/1817 |
| 517 | Lied: | *Der Schäfer und der Reiter*/April 1817/2 versions |
| 518 | Lied: | *An den Tod*/1816-1817 |
| 519 | Lied: | *Die Blumensprache*/1817 |
| 520 | Lied: | *Frohsinn*/January 1817/2 versions |
| 521 | Lied/Chorlied: | *Jagdlied*/January 1817 |
| 522 | Lied: | *Die Liebe*/January 1817 |
| 523 | Lied: | *Trost*/January 1817 |
| 524 | Lied: | *Der Alpenjäger*/January 1817/3 versions |

2/Deutsch catalogue/continued

525  Lied: *Wie Ulfru fischt*/January 1817/2 versions
526  Lied: *Fahrt zum Hades*/January 1817
527  Lied: *Schlaflied*/January 1817/2 versions
528  Arietta: *La pastorella al prato*/January 1817/second version
**529  8 Ecossaises/February 1817**
530  Lied: *An eine Quelle*/February 1817
531  Lied: *Der Tod und das Mädchen*/February 1817
532  Lied: *Das Lied vom Reifen*/February 1817
533  Lied: *Täglich zu singen*/February 1817
534  Lied: *Die Nacht*/February 1817
535  Lied with orchestra: *Brüder schrecklich brennt die Träne*
536  Lied: *Der Schiffer*/1817/2 versions
**537  Sonata in A minor/March 1817**
538  Vocal Quartet: *Gesang der Geister über den Wassern*/second version
539  Lied: *Am Strome*/March 1817
540  Lied: *Philoktet*/March 1817
541  Lied: *Memnon*/March 1817
542  Lied: *Antigone und Oedip*/March 1817
543  Lied: *Auf dem See*/March 1817/2 versions
544  Lied: *Ganymed*/March 1817
545  Lied: *Der Jüngling und der Tod*/March 1817/2 versions
546  Lied: *Trost im Liede*/March 1817/2 versions
547  Lied: *An die Musik*/March 1817/2 versions
548  Lied: *Orest auf Tauris*/March 1817
549  Lied: *Mahomets Gesang*/March 1817/first version/incomplete

*2/Deutsch catalogue/continued*

| | | |
|---|---|---|
| 550 | Lied: | *Die Forelle*/1816-1817/5 versions |
| 551 | Lied: | *Pax vobiscum*/April 1817 |
| 552 | Lied: | *Hänflings Liebeswerbung*/April 1817/2 versions |
| 553 | Lied: | *Auf der Donau*/April 1817 |
| 554 | Lied: | *Uraniens Flucht*/April 1817 |
| 555 | Sketch for a Lied without text/April 1817 | |
| 556 | Overture in D/May 1817 | |

**557 Sonata in A flat/May 1817**

558 Lied: *Liebhaber in allen Gestalten*/May 1817
559 Lied: *Schweizerlied*/May 1817
560 Lied: *Der Goldschmiedsgesell*/May 1817
561 Lied: *Nach einem Gewitter*/May 1817
562 Lied: *Fischerlied*/May 1817/third version
563 Lied: *Die Einsiedelei*/May 1817/third version
564 Lied: *Gretchen im Zwinger*/May 1817/incomplete
565 Lied: *Der Strom*/June 1817

**566 Sonata in E minor/June 1817**
**567 Sonata in D flat/June 1817**
**568 Sonata in E flat/June 1817**

569 Lied: *Das Grab*/June 1817/fourth version

**570 Scherzo in D and Allegro in F sharp/July 1817**
**571 Sonata in F sharp/July 1817/incomplete**

572 Vocal Quartet: *Lied im Freien*/July 1817
573 Lied: *Iphigenia*/July 1817/3 versions
574 Violin Sonata in A/August 1817

2/Deutsch catalogue/continued

| | | |
|---|---|---|
| **575** | **Sonata in B/August 1817** | |
| **576** | **13 Variations on a theme of Hüttenbrenner/August 1817** | |
| 577 | Lied: *Die Entzückung an Laura*/August 1817/incomplete | |
| 578 | Lied: *Abschied*/August 1817 | |
| 579 | Lied: *Der Knabe in der Wiege*/1817/2 versions | |
| 579a | Lied: *Vollendung*/September-October 1817 | |
| 579b | Lied: *Die Erde*/September-October 1817 | |
| 580 | Polonaise in B for violin and orchestra/September 1817 | |
| 581 | String Trio in B/September 1817/2 versions | |
| 582 | Lied: *Augenblicke im Elysium* | |
| 583 | Lied: *Gruppe aus dem Tartarus*/September 1817/second version | |
| 584 | Lied: *Elysium*/September 1817 | |
| 585 | Lied: *Atys*/September 1817 | |
| 586 | Lied: *Erlafsee*/September 1817 | |
| 587 | Lied: *An den Frühling*/October 1817/third version | |
| 588 | Lied: *Der Alpenjäger*/October 1817/2 versions | |
| 589 | Symphony in C/October 1817-February 1818 | |
| 590 | Overture in D in the Italian style/November 1817 | |
| 591 | Overture in C in the Italian style/November 1817 | |
| **592** | **Overture in D in the Italian style for 4 hands/December 1817** | |
| **593** | **2 Scherzi/November 1817** | |
| 594 | Lied: *Der Kampf*/November 1817 | |
| 595 | Lied: *Thekla*/November 1817/second version | |
| 596 | Lied: *Lied eines Kindes*/November 1817/incomplete | |
| **597** | **Overture in C in the Italian style for 4 hands/December 1817** | |
| 597a | Variations in A for violin/December 1817/lost sketch | |

*2/Deutsch catalogue/continued*

| | |
|---|---|
| 598 | Vocal Quartet: *Das Dörfchen*/December 1817/2 versions |
| 598a | Exercises for figured basses |
| **599** | **4 Polonaises for four hands/July 1818** |
| **600** | **Minuet in C sharp minor/1814** |
| 601 | Overture in B for string quartet |
| **602** | **3 Marches Heroiques for four hands/1818-1824** |
| **603** | **Introduction, Variations and Finale in B for four hands** |
| **604** | **Andante in A/1816-1817** |
| **605** | **Fantasy in C/1821-1823/incomplete** |
| **605a** | **Fantasy in C "Grazer Fantasie"/1818** |
| **606** | **March in E/1818** |
| 607 | Evangelium Johannis 6 for voice and figured bass/1818 |
| **608** | **Rondo in D for four hands/January 1818/2 versions** |
| 609 | Vocal Quartet: *Die Geselligkeit*/January 1818 |
| **610** | **Trio in E/February 1818** |
| 611 | Lied: *Auf der Riesenkoppe*/March 1818 |
| **612** | **Adagio in E/April 1818** |
| **613** | **Sonata in C/April 1818/incomplete** |
| 614 | Lied: *An den Mond*/April 1818 |
| 615 | Symphony in C/May 1818/sketch for two movements |
| 616 | Lied: *Grablied für die Mutter*/June 1818 |
| **617** | **Sonata in B for four hands/1818** |
| **618** | **Deutscher Tanz in G minor for four hands/1818** |
| **618a** | **Polonaise in B for four hands/July 1818/sketch** |
| 619 | Vocal Exercises with figured bass/July 1818 |
| 620 | Lied: *Einsamkeit*/July 1818 |

*2/Deutsch catalogue/continued*

621 Deutsches Requiem in G/August 1818
622 Lied: *Der Blumenbrief*/August 1818
623 Lied: *Das Marienbild*/August 1818
**624 8 Variations on a French song for 4 hands/September 1818**
**625 Sonata in F minor/September 1818/incomplete**
626 Lied: *Blondel zu Marien*/September 1818
627 Lied: *Das Abendrot*/November 1818
628 Lied: *Apollo lebet noch dein hold Verlangen*/November 1818
629 Lied: *Allein nachdenklich*/November 1818
630 Lied: *Nunmehr da Himmel Erde schweiget*/December 1818
631 Lied: *Blanka (Das Mädchen)*/December 1818
632 Lied: *Vom Mitleiden Mariä*/December 1818
633 Lied: *Der Schmetterling*/1819-1823
634 Lied: *Die Berge*/1819-1823
635 Vocal Quartet: *Leise leise lasst uns singen*/1819
636 Lied: *Sehnsucht*/1821/second version
637 Lied: *Hoffnung*/1819/second version
638 Lied: *Der Jüngling am Bache*/April 1819/third version
639 Lied: *Widerschein*/September 1820/2 versions
**640 2 Tänze/sketches**
641 Vocal Quartet: *Das Dörfchen*/second version
642 Vocal Quartet: *Viel tausend Sterne prangen*/1812
**643 Deutscher Tanz in C sharp minor & Ecossaise in D flat/1819**
643a Vocal Quartet: *Das Grab*/1819/fifth version
644 Zauberspiel mit Musik: *Die Zauberharfe*/1820
645 Lied: *Abend*/1819/incomplete sketch
646 Lied: *Die Gebüsche*/January 1819
647 Singspiel: *Die Zwillingsbrüder*/January 1819
648 Overture in E/February 1819
649 Lied: *Der Wanderer*/February 1819/2 versions

*2/Deutsch catalogue/continued*

650 Lied: *Abendbilder*/February 1819
651 Lied: *Himmelsfunken*/February 1819
652 Lied: *Das Mädchen*/February 1819/2 versions
653 Lied: *Bertas Lied in der Nacht*/February 1819
654 Lied: *An die Freunde*/March 1819
**655 Sonata in C sharp/April 1819/incomplete**
656 Vocal Quintet: *Sehnsucht*/April 1819/fourth version
657 Vocal Quartet: *Ruhe schönstes Glück der Erde*/April 1819
658 Lied: *Marie (Ich sehe dich in tausend Bildern)*/May 1819
659 Lied: *Hymne I*/May 1819
660 Lied: *Hymne II*/May 1819
661 Lied: *Hymne III*/May 1819
662 Lied: *Hymne IV*/May 1819
663 Lied: *Der 13. Psalm*/June 1819/incomplete
**664 Sonata in A/1819-1825**
665 Vocal Quartet: *Im traulichen Kreise*/incomplete
666 Vocal Trio: *Kantate zum Geburtstag von J.M.Vogl*/August 1819
667 Piano Trio in A "Die Forelle"/1819
**668 Overture in G for 4 hands/October 1819**
669 Lied: *Beim Winde*/October 1819
670 Lied: *Die Sternennächte*/October 1819
671 Lied: *Trost*/October 1819
672 Lied: *Nachtstück*/October 1819/2 versions
673 Lied: *Die Liebende schreibt*/October 1819
674 Lied: *Prometheus (Bedecke deinen Himmel Zeus)*/October 1819

*2/Deutsch catalogue/continued*

**675  Overture in F for 4 hands/November 1819**
676  Salve regina in F/November 1819
677  Lied: *Strophe aus "Die Götter Griechenlands"*/1819/2 versions
678  Mass in A flat/1819-1822
**679  2 Ländler in E flat**
**680  2 Ländler in D flat**
**681  12 Ländler/1815/numbers 1-4 lost**
682  Lied: *Ueber allen Zauber Liebe*/1820-1824/incomplete
683  Aria: *Die Wolkenbraut (Alfonso und Estrella)*
684  Lied: *Die Sterne*/1820
685  Lied: *Morgenlied*/1820
686  Lied: *Frühlingsglaube*/September 1820/3 versions
687  Lied: *Nachthymne*/January 1820
688  4 Kanzonen für eine Singstimme/January 1820
689  Scenic Oratorio: *Lazarus*/February 1820/incomplete
690  Lied: *Abendröte*/March 1820
691  Lied: *Die Vögel*/March 1820
692  Lied: *Der Knabe*/March 1820
693  Lied: *Der Fluss*/March 1820
694  Lied: *Der Schiffer*/March 1820
695  Lied: *Namenstagslied*/March 1820
696  6 Antiphonen zum Palmsonntag/March 1820
**697  6 Ecossaises in A flat/May 1820**
698  Lied: *Des Fräuleins Liebeslauschen*/September 1820
699  Lied: *Der entsühnte Orest*/September 1820

2/Deutsch catalogue/continued

| | | |
|---|---|---|
| 700 | Lied: | *Freiwilliges Versinken*/September 1820 |
| 701 | Oper: | *Sakuntala*/October 1820/incomplete |
| 702 | Lied: | *Der Jüngling auf dem Hügel*/November 1820 |
| 703 | String Quartet in C/December 1820/incomplete | |
| 704 | Vocal Octet: | *Gesang der Geister über den Wassern* |
| 705 | Vocal Quartet: | *Gesang der Geister über den Wassern* |
| 706 | Vocal Quartet: | *Der 23. Psalm*/December 1820 |
| 707 | Lied: | *Der zürnenden Diana*/December 1820/2 versions |
| 708 | Lied: | *Im Walde*/December 1820 |
| 708a | Symphony in D/1820/sketches | |
| 709 | Vocal Quartet: | *Frühlingsgesang*/April 1822 |
| 710 | Vocal Quartet: | *Im Gegenwärtigen Vergangenes*/March 1821 |
| 711 | Lied: | *Lob der Tränen*/1818/2 versions |
| 712 | Lied: | *Die gefangenen Sänger*/January 1821 |
| 713 | Lied: | *Der Unglückliche*/January 1821/2 versions |
| 714 | Vocal Octet: | *Gesang der Geister über den Wassern* |
| 715 | Lied: | *Versunken*/February 1821 |
| 716 | Lied: | *Grenzen der Menschheit*/March 1821 |
| 717 | Lied: | *Suleika II*/March 1821 |
| **718** | **Variation in C on a waltz by Diabelli/March 1821** | |
| 719 | Lied: | *Geheimes*/March 1821 |
| 720 | Lied: | *Suleika I*/March 1821/2 versions |
| 721 | Lied: | *Mahomets Gesang*/March 1821/second version |
| **722** | **Deutscher Tanz in G flat/March 1821** | |
| 723 | Duet and Aria for Herold's *Das Zauberglöckchen*/June 1821 | |
| 724 | Vocal Quartet: | *Die Nachtigall*/April 1821 |

*2/Deutsch catalogue/continued*

725 Vocal Duet: *Linde Weste wehen*/April 1821
726 Lied: *Heiss mich nicht reden*/April 1821/first version
727 Lied: *So lasst mich scheinen*/April 1821/second version
728 Lied: *Johanna Sebus*/April 1821/incomplete
729 Symphony in E/August 1821
730 Tantum ergo in B/August 1821
731 Lied: *Der Blumen Schmerz*/September 1821
732 Oper: *Alfonso und Estrella*/September 1821-February 1822
**733 3 Marches militaires for 4 hands/1818**
**734 16 Ländler and 2 Ecossaises/December 1826**
**735 Galopp and 8 Ecossaises/November 1825**
736 Lied: *Ihr Grab*/1822
737 Lied: *An die Leier*/1822-1823
738 Lied: *Im Haine*/1822-1823
739 Tantum ergo in C/1814
740 Vocal Quartet: *Frühlingsgesang*/January-April 1822
741 Lied: *Sei mir gegrüsst*/1821-1822
742 Lied: *Der Wachtelschlag*/July 1822
743 Lied: *Selige Welt*/1822
744 Lied: *Schwanengesang*/1822
745 Lied: *Die Rose*/1822/2 versions
746 Lied: *Am See*/1822-1823
747 Vocal Quartet: *Geist der Liebe*/January 1822/second version
748 Kantate: *Am Geburtstage des Kaisers*/January 1822
749 Lied: *Herrn Josef Spaun*/January 1822

2/Deutsch catalogue/continued

750 Tantum ergo in D/March 1822
751 Lied: *Die Liebe hat gelogen*/April 1822
752 Lied: *Nachtviolen*/April 1822
753 Lied: *Heliopolis I*/April 1822
754 Lied: *Heliopolis II*/April 1822
755 Kyrie for a Mass in A/May 1822/sketch
756 Lied: *Du liebst mich nicht*/July 1822/2 versions
757 Vocal Quartet: *Gott in der Natur*/August 1822
758 Lied: *Todesmusik*/September 1822
759 Symphony in B minor "Unfinished"/October 1822
**759a Overture "Alfonso & Estrella" for 4 hands/November 1822**
**760 Fantasy in C "Wanderer"/November 1822**
761 Lied: *Schatzgräbers Begehr*/November 1822/2 versions
762 Lied: *Schwestergruss*/November 1822
763 Vocal Quartet: *Des Tages Weihe*/November 1822
764 Lied: *Der Musensohn*/December 1822/2 versions
765 Lied: *An die Entfernte*/December 1822
766 Lied: *Am Flusse*/December 1822/second version
767 Lied: *Willkommen und Abschied*/December 1822/2 versions
768 Lied: *Wanderers Nachtlied*/May 1824
**769 2 Deutsche Tänze in A and D/1823-1824**
**769a Sonata in E/1823/incomplete**
770 Lied: *Drang in die Ferne*/1823
771 Lied: *Der Zwerg*/1822
772 Lied: *Wehmut*/1822-1823
**773 Overture to "Alfonso und Estrella" for 4 hands**
774 Lied: *Auf dem Wasser zu singen*/1823

2/Deutsch catalogue/continued

| | | |
|---|---|---|
| 775 | Lied: | *Dass sie hier gewesen*/1826 |
| 776 | Lied: | *Du bist die Ruh*/1823 |
| 777 | Lied: | *Lachen und Weinen*/1823 |
| 778 | Lied: | *Greisengesang*/1823/3 versions |
| 778a | Lied: | *Die Wallfahrt*/1823 |
| 778b | Vocal Quartet: | *Ich hab in mich gesogen*/1827/sketch |
| **779** | **34 Valses sentimentales/1825** | |
| **780** | **6 Moments musicaux/1823-1824** | |
| **781** | **Ecossaises/January 1823** | |
| **782** | **Ecossaise in D/February 1824** | |
| **783** | **16 Deutsche Tänze and 2 Ecossaises/1823-1825** | |
| **784** | **Sonata in A minor/February 1823** | |
| 785 | Lied: | *Der zürnende Barde*/February 1823 |
| 786 | Lied: | *Viola*/March 1823 |
| 787 | Singspiel: | *Die Verschworenen*/April 1823 |
| 788 | Lied: | *Die Mutter Erde*/April 1823 |
| 789 | Lied: | *Pilgerweise*/April 1823 |
| **790** | **12 Deutsche Tänze/May 1823** | |
| 791 | Oper: | *Rüdiger*/May 1823/incomplete sketches |
| 792 | Lied: | *Vergissmeinnicht*/May 1823 |
| 793 | Lied: | *Das Geheimnis*/May 1823/second version |
| 794 | Lied: | *Der Pilgrim*/May 1823/2 versions |
| 795 | Lied-Zyklus: | *Die schöne Müllerin*/October-November 1823 |
| 796 | Oper: | *Fierabras*/May-October 1823 |
| 797 | Schauspiel mit Musik: | *Rosamunde*/1823 |
| **798** | **Overture to "Fierabras" for 4 hands/1826-1827** | |
| 799 | Lied: | *Im* Abendrot/1824-1825 |

*2/Deutsch catalogue/continued*

| | | |
|---|---|---|
| 800 | Lied: *Der Einsame*/1825 | |
| 801 | Lied: *Dithyrambe*/June 1826/2 versions | |
| 802 | Variations on "Trockne Blumen" for flute & piano/1824 | |
| 803 | Octet in F/February-March 1824 | |
| 804 | String Quartet in A/February-March 1824 | |
| 805 | Lied: *Der Sieg*/March 1824 | |
| 806 | Lied: *Abendstern*/March 1824 | |
| 807 | Lied: *Auflösung*/March 1824 | |
| 808 | Lied: *Gondelfahrer*/March 1824 | |
| 809 | Vocal Quartet: *Gondelfahrer*/1824 | |
| 810 | String Quartet in D "Der Tod und das Mädchen"/1824 | |
| 811 | Salve regina in C/April 1824 | |
| 812 | **Sonata in C for 4 hands  "Grand Duo"/June 1824** | |
| 813 | **8 Variations in A flat for 4 hands/May-July 1824** | |
| 814 | **4 Ländler for 4 hands/July 1824** | |
| 815 | Vocal Quartet: *Gebet*/September 1824 | |
| 816 | **3 Ecossaises/September 1824** | |
| 817 | **Ungarische Melodie in F/September 1824** | |
| 818 | **Divertissement a la hongroise for 4 hands/1824** | |
| 819 | **6 Grandes Marches et Trios for 4 hands/1818-1824** | |
| 820 | **6 Deutsche Tänze/October 1824** | |
| 821 | Sonata for Cello and Piano  "Arpeggione"/November 1824 | |
| 822 | Lied: *Lied eines Kriegers*/December 1824 | |
| 823 | **Divertissement a la francais for 4 hands/1826-1827** | |
| 824 | **6 Polonaises for 4 hands/April-July 1826** | |

*2/Deutsch catalogue/continued*

| | | |
|---|---|---|
| 825 | Vocal Quartet: | *Wehmut*/1826 |
| 825a | Vocal Quartet: | *Ewige Liebe*/1826 |
| 825b | Vocal Quartet: | *Flucht*/1825 |
| 826 | Vocal Quartet: | *Der Tanz*/1828 |
| 827 | Lied: | *Nacht und Träume*/June 1823/2 versions |
| 828 | Lied: | *Die junge Nonne*/1825 |
| 829 | Melodram: | *Abschied*/1826 |
| 830 | Lied: | *Lied der Anne Lyle*/1825 |
| 831 | Lied: | *Gesang der Norna*/1825 |
| 832 | Lied: | *Des Sängers Habe*/February 1825 |
| 833 | Lied: | *Der blinde Knabe*/April 1825/2 versions |
| 834 | Lied: | *Im Walde*/March 1825/2 versions |
| 835 | Vocal Quartet: | *Bootgesang*/1825 |
| 836 | Chorlied: | *Coronach*/1825 |
| 837 | Lied: | *Ellens Gesang I*/April-July 1825 |
| 838 | Lied: | *Ellens Gesang II*/April-July 1825 |
| 839 | Lied: | *Ellens Gesang III*/April 1825 |
| **840** | **Sonata in C/April 1825** | |
| **841** | **2 Deutsche Tänze/April 1825** | |
| 842 | Lied: | *Totengräbers Heimweh*/April 1825 |
| 843 | Lied: | *Lied des gefangenen Jägers*/April 1825 |
| **844** | **Waltz in G (Albumblatt)/April 1825** | |

*2/Deutsch catalogue/continued*

| | |
|---|---|
| **845** | **Sonata in A minor/May 1825** |
| 846 | Lied: *Normans Gesang*/April 1825 |
| 847 | Vocal Quartet: *Trinklied*/July 1825 |
| 848 | Vocal Quartet: *Nachtmusik*/July 1825 |
| 849 | Symphony/June-September 1825/lost |
| **850** | **Sonata in D/August 1825** |
| 851 | Lied: *Das Heimweh*/August 1825/2 versions |
| 852 | Lied: *Die Allmacht*/August 1825/first version |
| 853 | Lied: *Auf der Bruck*/1825/2 versions |
| 854 | Lied: *Fülle der Liebe*/August 1825 |
| 855 | Lied: *Wiedersehn*/September 1825 |
| 856 | Lied: *Abendlied für die Entfernte*/September 1825 |
| 857 | 2 Szenen aus dem Schauspiel "Lacrimas"/September 1825 |
| **858** | **March for 8 hands/lost** |
| **859** | **Grande marche funebre for 4 hands/December 1825** |
| 860 | Lied: *An mein Herz*/December 1825 |
| 861 | Lied: *Der liebliche Stern*/December 1825 |
| 862 | Lied: *Um Mitternacht*/December 1825/2 versions |
| 863 | Lied: *An Gott*/1827/lost |
| 864 | Lied: *Das Totenhemdchen*/1825/lost |
| 865 | Chorlied: *Widerspruch*/1828 |
| 866 | 4 Refrainlieder/1828 |
| 867 | Lied: *Wiegenlied*/1828 |
| 868 | Lied: *Das Echo* |
| 869 | Lied: *Totengräberweise*/1826 |
| 870 | Lied: *Der Wanderer an den Mond*/1826 |
| 871 | Lied: *Das Zügenglöcklein*/1826/2 versions |
| 872 | Deutsche Messe/1827 |
| 873 | Canon for 6 voices/January 1826/sketch |
| 873a | Vocal Quartet: *Nachklänge*/January 1826/sketch |
| 874 | Lied: *O Quell was strömst du?*/1826/sketch |

*2/Deutsch catalogue/continued*

875 Vocal Quintet: *Mondenschein*/January 1826
875a Chorlied: *Die Allmacht*/January 1826/second version/sketch
876 Lied: *Im Jänner 1817*/January 1826
877 Lieder: 4 Gesänge aus Wilhelm Meister/January 1826
878 Lied: *Am Fenster*/March 1826
879 Lied: *Sehnsucht*/March 1826
880 Lied: *Im Freien*/March 1826
881 Lied: *Fischerweise*/March 1826/2 versions
882 Lied: *Im Frühling*/March 1826/2 versions
883 Lied: *Lebensmut*/March 1826
884 Lied: *Ueber Wildemann*/March 1826
**885 Grande marche heroique in A for 4 hands/1825-1826**
**886 2 Marches caracteristiques in C for 4 hands**
887 String Quartet in G/June 1826
888 Lied: *Trinklied*/July 1826
889 Lied: *Horch horch die Lerch!*/July 1826
890 Lied: *Hippolits Lied*/July 1826
891 Lied: *Was ist Sylvia saget an?*/July 1826
892 Lied für Tenor und Quartett: *Nachthelle*/September 1826
893 Vocal Quartet: *Grab und Mond*/September 1826
**894 Sonata in G/October 1826**
895 Rondo for violin and orchestra/October 1826
896 Lied: *Fröhliches Scheiden*/1827-1828/sketch
896b Lied: *Sie in jedem Liede*/1827-1828/sketch
897 Notturno for piano, violin and cello/1828
898 Trio for piano, violin and cello/1828
**899 4 Impromptus/1827**

*2/Deutsch catalogue/continued*

**900 Allegretto in C/1822-1823/incomplete**
901 Vocal Quartet: *Wein und Liebe*/1827
902 3 Gesänge für Bass/1827
903 Chorlied: *Zur guten Nacht*/January 1827
904 Lied: *Alinde*/January 1827
905 Lied: *An die Laute*/January 1827
906 Lied: *Der Vater mit dem Kind*/January 1827
907 Lied: *Romanze des Richard Löwenherz*/March 1826/2 versions
**908 8 Variations on a theme from Herold's "Marie" for 4 hands/1827**
909 Lied: *Jägers Liebeslied*/February 1827
910 Lied: *Schiffers Scheidelied*/February 1827
911 Lied-Zyklus: *Die Winterreise*/February-October 1827
912 Chorlied: *Schlachtlied*/February 1827/second version
913 Vocal Quartet: *Nachtgesang im Walde*/April 1827
914 Vocal Quartet: *Frühlingslied*/April 1827/first version
**915 Allegretto in C/April 1827**
916 Vocal Quartet: *Das stille Lied*/May 1827
916a Lied sketch without text/May 1827/incomplete
**916b Klavierstück in C/1827/incomplete**
**916c Klavierstück in C/1827/incomplete**
917 Lied: *Das Lied im Grünen*/June 1827
918 Oper: *Der Graf von Gleichen*/June 1827/incomplete sketches
919 Lied: *Frühlingslied*/1827/second version

2/Deutsch catalogue/continued

920 Chorlied mit Alt-Solo: *Zögernd leise*/July 1827/first version
921 Chorlied mit Alt-Solo: *Zögernd leise*/July 1826/second version
922 Lied: *Heimliches Lieben*/September 1827/2 versions
923 Lied: *Altschottische Ballade*/September 1827/3 versions
**924 12 Grazer Walzer/September 1827**
**925 Grazer Galopp/September 1827**
926 Lied: *Das Weinen*/April 1828
927 Lied: *Vor meiner Wiege*/1827-1828
**928 Kindermarsch in G minor for 4 hands/October 1827**
929 Trio in E flat for piano, violin and cello/November 1827
930 Vocal Trio: *Der Hochzeitsbraten*/November 1827
931 Lied: *Der Wallensteiner Lanzknecht beim Trunk*/November 1827
932 Lied: *Der Kreuzzug*/November 1827
933 Lied: *Des Fischers Liebesglück*/November 1827
934 Fantasy in C for violin and piano/December 1827
**935 4 Impromptus/December 1827**
936 Vocal Quartet: *Kantate für Irene Kiesewetter*/December 1827
936a Symphony in D/1828/sketches
937 Lied: *Lebensmut*/1828/incomplete
938 Lied: *Der Winterabend*/January 1828
939 Lied: *Die Sterne*/January 1828
**940 Fantasy in F for 4 hands/January-April 1828**
941 Vocal Quartet: *Hymnus an den heiligen Geist*/first version
942 Kantate: *Mirjams Siegesgesang*/March 1828
943 Lied: *Auf dem Strom*/March 1828
944 Symphony in C "Grosse"/1825-1828

*2/Deutsch catalogue/continued*

**944a Deutscher Tanz/March 1828/lost**
945    Lied: *Herbst*/April 1828
**946    3 Klavierstücke/May 1828**
**947    Allegro in A for 4 hands "Lebensstürme"/May 1828**
948    Vocal Quartet: *Hymnus an den heiligen Geist*/second version
949    Lied: *Widerschein*/second version
950    Mass in E flat/June 1828
**951    Grand rondeau in A for 4 hands/June 1828**
**952    Fugue in E for 4 hands/June 1828**
953    Chorlied: *Der 92. Psalm*/July 1828
954    Vocal Quartet: *Glaube Hoffnung und Liebe*/August 1828
955    Lied: *Glaube Hoffnung und Liebe*/August 1828
956    String Quintet in C/September 1828
957    Lied-Zyklus: *Schwanengesang*/1828
**958    Sonata in C minor/September 1828**
**959    Sonata in A/September 1828**
**960    Sonata in B flat/September 1828**
961    Benedictus for Mass in C/second version
962    Tantum ergo in E flat/October 1828
963    Arie mit Chor: *Intende voci orationis meae*/October 1828

*2/Deutsch catalogue/continued*

964 Vocal Quartet: *Hymnus an den heiligen Geist*/second version
965 Lied mit Klarinette: *Der Hirt auf dem Felsen*
965a Lied: *Die Taubenpost*/October 1828
965b Fugal Exercises/November 1828
966 Orchestral Interlude from "Der Spiegelritter"
966a Orchesterstück in D/August-September 1813/incomplete
966b Orchesterstück in A/sketches
**967 Fugal Sketches/1813**
**968 Allegro and Andante for 4 hands**
**968a Introduction and Variations in B for 4 hands**
**968b 2 Marches caracteristiques in C for 4 hands**
**969 12 Walzer "Valses nobles"**
**970 6 Ländler**
**971 3 Deutsche Tänze**
**972 3 Deutsche Tänze**
**973 3 Deutsche Tänze**
**974 2 Deutsche in D flat**
**975 Deutscher in D**
**976 Cotillon in E flat**
**977 8 Ecossaises**
**978 Walzer in A flat**
**979 Walzer in G**
**980 2 Walzer**
**980a 2 Sketches for Dances**
**980b 2 Ländler in E flat**
**980c 2 Ländler in D flat**

*2/Deutsch catalogue/continued*

**980d**   **Walzer in C**
**980e**   **2 Sketches for Dances**
**980f**   **March in G**
981   Singspiel: *Der Minnesänger*/lost
982   Sketches for an opera
983   Vocal Quartet: *Jünglingswonne*
983a   Vocal Quartet: *Liebe*
983b   Vocal Quartet: *Zum Rundetanz*
983c   Vocal Quartet: *Die Nacht*
984   Vocal Quartet: *Der Wintertag*
985   Vocal Quartet: *Gott im Ungewitter*
986   Vocal Quartet: *Gott der Weltschöpfer*
987   Chorlied: *Jesus Christus unser Heiland*/1815
988   Canon: *Liebe säuseln die Blätter*
988a   Lied accompaniment without title or text
989   Lied: *Vollendung*/1817
989a   Lied: *Die Erde*/1817

*2/Deutsch catalogue/concluded*

| | |
|---|---|
| 990 | Lied: *Der Graf von Habsburg* |
| 990a | Lied: *Kaiser Maximilian auf der Martinswand* |
| 990b | Lied: *Augenblicke im Elysium*/lost |
| 990c | Lied: *Das Echo* |
| 990d | Lied: *Die Schiffende*/lost |
| 990e | Aria: *L'incanto degli occhi*/incomplete |
| 990f | Aria: *Il traditor deluso*/incomplete |
| 991 | Lied: *So lasst euch froh begrüssen*/incomplete |
| 992 | Aria: *Wer wird sich nicht innig freuen*/sketch |
| **993** | **Fantasy in C/1811** |
| **994** | **Sonata in E/1823** |
| 995 | 6 Minuets for wind/1811 |
| 996 | Overture in D/1811 |
| 997 | Symphony in D/1811 |
| 998 | String Quartet movement/1811/incomplete |

*Deutsch numbers 967-998 are items added to the original catalogue which cannot be precisely dated*

## FRANZ SCHUBERT: THE PIANO SONATAS

### 3A: COMPLETE OR NEAR-COMPLETE SETS
*Including incomplete and re-constructed works*

**Martino Tirimo (20+ sonatas)**
D157, D279/346, D459, D537, D557, D566/506, D568, D570/571/604, D575, D613/612, D625/505, D664, D784, D840, D845, D850, D894, D958, D959, D960, D567, D655 fragment, D769a fragment
CD: Warner Classics 846 8522
*Recorded in St Philips Church Norbury and Forde Abbey Dorset between November 1995-July 1996*

**Paul Badura-Skoda (20 Sonatas)**
D157, D279/346, D459, D537, D557, D566/506, D568, D570/571/604, D575, D613/612, D625/505, D664, D784, D840, D845, D850, D894, D958, D959, D960
CD: Arcana A 364
*Recorded in Vienna Palais Clam-Gallos, Baumgartner Casino and Zögernitz Casino between January 1991-April 1996*

**Paul Badura-Skoda (20 Sonatas)**
D157, D279/346, D459, D537, D557, D566/506, D568, D571/604/570, D575, D612/D613, D625/605, D664, D784, D840, D845, D850, D894, D958, D959, D960
LP: RCA Victor SRA 2661-2673/SCH 1
*Published in 1971*

*3a/complete or near-complete sets/continued*

**Andras Schiff (19 Sonatas)**
D157, D279, D459, D537, D557, D566, D568,
D571, D575, D625, D664, D784, D840, D845,
D850, D894, D958, D959, D960
CD: Decca 448 3092/478 3018
*Recorded between 1993-1996*

**Friedrich Wührer (18 Sonatas)**
D157, D279/346, D459, D537, D557, D566/506,
D568, D575, D625/505, D664, D784, D840, D845,
D850, D894, D958, D959, D960
LP: Vox PL 8210/PL 8240/PL 8420/PL 9130/PL 9620/
VBX 10/VBX 11
CD: Bearac BRC 2980/BRC 2981/BRC 8291/
CRQ Editions CRQCD 138-139/CRQCD 197-198/
CRQCD 217-218
*Recorded in Vienna Konzerthaus between 1952-1955*

**Dieter Zechlin (18 Sonatas)**
D157, D279/346, D459, D537, D557, D566/605,
D568, D575, D625/505, D664, D784, D840,
D845, D850, D894, D958, D959, D960
LP: Eterna
CD: Berlin Classics 018 4482BC
*Recorded in Dresden Lukaskirche and Berlin-Ost Studio Brunnenstrasse between September 1970-February 1976*

*3a/complete or near-complete sets/continued*
**Wilhelm Kempff (18 Sonatas)**
D157, D279/346, D459, D537, D557, D566/506,
D568, D575, D625/505, D664, D784, D840,
D845, D850, D894, D958, D959, D960
LP: Deutsche Grammophon 2740 132
CD: Deutsche Grammophon 463 7662
*Recorded in Hannover Beethovensaal between February 1965-January 1969*

**Michael Endres (17 Sonatas)**
D157, D279/346, D537, D557, D566/506, D568,
D575, D613/612, D625/505, D664, D784, D840,
D845, D850, D894, D958, D959, D960
CD: Capriccio C 7125
*Recorded in Cologne WDR Funkhaus between December 1993-July 1997*

**Gerhard Oppitz (17 Sonatas)**
D157, D279/346, D459, D537, D557, D566/606,
D568, D575, D664, D784, D840, D845, D850,
D894, D958, D959, D960
CD: Hänssler Classics
*Recorded in Neumarkt/Oberpfalz Historischer Reitstadel between May 2007-October 2009*

*3a/complete or near complete sets/concluded*

*My personal preference among these complete or near-complete sets lies with Dieter Zechlin (captured by the East German engineers in bright studio sound) or the Viennese Friedrich Wührer (albeit in the less consistent sound quality of 1950s Vox pressings). Wilhelm Kempff can claim to have been the first to record the Schubert Sonatas as an integral cycle (although certain sonatas from the set were issued on individual LPs prior to publication of the boxed set), but already in the 1950s Kempff had recorded D845 and D960 for the British Decca label. Badura-Skoda's important project from the 1990s, using the fortepiano, will not be to the taste of those who prefer the sound of the modern grand; Badura-Skoda's earlier LP cycle for RCA in 1971 has so far eluded me, but even before that he had already made considerable contribution to the recorded Schubert piano literature for a variety of labels starting as early as the 1950s. Sadly, the most complete set of all, that of Martino Tirimo, comes in a sound quality hardly acceptable for a studio production of the 1990s – the impression is, to my ears, of an amateur effort with hand-held microphone.*

## 3B: STANDARD COMPLETE SETS

*Containing the Sonatas considered to exist fully completed at the time of recording*

**Ingrid Haebler (12 Sonatas)**
D459, D537, D568, D575, D664, D784, D845, D850, D894, D958, D959, D960
LP: Philips 6741 002
CD: Philips 456 3672/478 5859/
Decca (Korea) DN 0021
*Recorded in Salzburg Mozarteum, Berlin Johannestift and in Eindhoven between October 1967-March 1970*

**Mitsuko Uchida (12 Sonatas)**
D537, D568, D575, D664, D784, D840, D845, D850, D894, D958, D959, D960
CD: Decca 475 6282

**Daniel Barenboim (11 Sonatas)**
D537, D568, D575, D664, D784, D845, D850, D894, D958, D959, D960
CD: Deutsche Grammophon 479 2783
*Recorded in Berlin Teldex Studio between January 2013-February 2014*

*3B/Standard complete sets/concluded*

**Alfred Brendel (11 Sonatas)**
D537, D575, D664, D784, D840, D845,
D850, D894, D958, D959, D960
LP: Philips 6747 175 (D784 onwards)
CD: Decca 480 1218
*Recorded between 1971-1982; later recordings by Brendel are listed under the individual works*

**Christian Zacharias (11 Sonatas)**
D537, D557, D575, D664, D784, D845,
D850, D894, D958, D959, D960
CD: EMI 565 4832

**Radu Lupu (9 Sonatas)**
D157, D557, D664, D784, D845,
D894, D958, D959, D960
CD: Decca
*Recorded in London, Hamburg and Corseaux between March 1970-December 1991*

*My clear personal recommendation for a set of the standard completed sonatas is for that of Ingrid Haebler in the clear studio sound for which Philips was noted in its piano recordings during the LP era: here are interpretations entirely without affectation but with the essential Viennese "Gemütlichkeit", a quality already expounded two decades earlier by Friedrich Wührer*

## 3C: A SPECIAL CASE

**Sviatoslav Richter (11 Sonatas)**
D566/506, D575, D625/505, D664, D784,
D840, D845, D850, D894, D958, D960
*Recorded in various locations for a variety of different labels over a period of 26 years, these important recordings nevertheless deserve consideration as an entity*


## 3D: LATE SONATAS
*Sonatas composed between 1817-1828*
**Elisabeth Leonskaya (9 Sonatas)**
D664, D784, D840, D845, D850,
D894, D958, D959, D960
CD: Easonus EAS 29300
*Recorded in 2015 in Berlin Meistersaal*

**Elisabeth Leonskaja (7 Sonatas)**
D568, D664, D850, D894, D958, D959, D960
CD: Warner Classics
*Recorded in Berlin Teldec Studios between 1988-1997*

**Paul Lewis (7 Sonatas)**
D784, D840, D850, D894, D958, D959, D960
CD: Harmonia mundi
*Recorded in London and Berlin between 2001-2011*

# FRANZ SCHUBERT: THE PIANO SONATAS

## 4: THE INDIVIDUAL SONATAS

**Sonata in E  D157**/*composed around February 1815*
Allegro ma non troppo
Andante
Menuetto-Allegro vivace

*Versions auditioned*
Paul Badura-Skoda (complete set)
Michael Endres (complete set)
Wilhelm Kempff  (complete set)
Arcadi Volodos  (Sony SK 89647)
Dieter Zechlin  (complete set)

*This incomplete torso,  lacking its final movement, exudes a Haydesque delight,  added to which Arcadi Volodos brings playing of a verve which also recalls a strong influence from Rossini*

4/Individual Sonatas/continued
**Sonata in C  D279/**composed around September 1815
Allegro moderato
Andante
Menuetto-Allegro vivace

*Versions auditioned*
Paul Badura-Skoda  (complete set)
Michael Endres  (complete set)
Wilhelm Kempff  (complete set)
Dieter Zechlin  (complete set)

*Hard not to conclude that Schubert had in mind Beethoven's epigrammatic op 49 Sonatas when composing this piece; again also a three-movement torso, Badura-Skoda adds the Allegretto D346 as a fourth movement, marred only by some jarring fortissimo chords from his fortepiano*

4/Individual Sonatas/continued

**Sonata in E  D459/D459a  (5 Klavierstücke)/**
*composed around August 1816*
Allegro moderato
Scherzo-Allegro
Adagio
Scherzo con trio-Allegro
Allegro patetico

*Versions auditioned*
Paul Badura-Skoda  (complete set)
Ingrid Haebler  (complete set)
Wilhelm Kempff  (complete set)
Dieter Zechlin  (complete set)

*The suggested origin of these five movements is of individual Klavierstücke:  they are certainly more rhapsodic in quality than the movements of the two previous sonatas,  and look forward to the later sets of Klavierstücke and Impromptus. The so-called Sonata is the earliest work to be included in Haebler's set of the "completed" ones, and she delivers a finely poised rendition of it.*

4/*Individual Sonatas/continued*

**Sonata in A minor D537**/*composed around March 1817*
Allegro ma non troppo
Allegretto quasi Andantino
Allegro vivace

*Versions auditioned*
Paul Badura-Skoda  (complete set)
Daniel Barenboim  (standard complete set)
Alfred Brendel  (standard complete set)
Michael Endres  (complete set)
Ingrid Haebler  (standard complete set)
Wilhelm Kempff  (complete set)
Arturo Benedetti Michelangeli  (DG 469 8202)
Eldar Nebolsin  (Naxos 8.572459)
Friedrich Wührer  (complete set)
Dieter Zechlin  (complete set)

*This is the earliest work in the cycle to be considered worthy of inclusion by those pianists who opt only for the standard set: of these, Barenboim and Brendel offer impeccably poised renditions, but it is left to Michelangeli, in his only Schubert on record, to plunge depths which encompass Beethovenian grandeur in the first movement and lyricism in the second (this movement is one of many in Schubert which either draws on, or anticipates, the world of his Lieder, in this case "Das Lied im Grünen" and "Im Frühling")*

*4/Individual Sonatas/continued*
**Sonata in A flat D557**/*composed around May 1817*
Allegro moderato
Andante
Allegro

*Versions auditioned*
Michael Endres (complete set)
Wilhelm Kempff (complete set)
Radu Lupu (standard complete set)

*This is the last of Schubert's sonatas to directly reflect the legacy of the triumvirate Haydn-Mozart-Beethoven. Concise in form, but with a second movement in that walking gait so characteristic of the composer, and then a final third movement with the inescapable dance-like impetus which is to be found in so many later Schubert works. The famed Kingsway Hall acoustic certainly adds lustre to Lupu's interpretation in this the first sonata in his "selective" complete cycle.*

4/Individual Sonatas/continued
**Sonata in E minor D566/D 506/**/composed around June 1817/
Moderato
Allegretto

*Versions auditioned*
Paul Badura-Skoda (complete cycle)
Wilhelm Kempff (complete cycle)
Sviatoslav Richter (versions from Aldeburgh, Munich and Moscow)
Dieter Zechlin (complete cycle)

*Kempff and Zechlin give us this two-movement torso, whereas Badura-Skoda and Richter add the Rondo-Allegretto D506 which already looks forward to the Scherzo of the Great C Major Symphony.*

*At this stage I should perhaps warn the reader that whenever the name of Richter occurs in this survey, all competition, however accomplished, will fade into the background. The manic strand in Richter's musical personality strikes me as bringing out precisely the same quality in Schubert's oeuvre (or at least in the limited number of Sonatas which he chose to explore in his public performances).*

4/Individual Sonatas/continued

**Sonata in E Flat  D568**/*completed around June 1817*

Allegro moderato
Andante molto
Menuetto-Allegretto
Allegro moderato

*Versions auditioned*
Paul Badura-Skoda  (complete set)
Daniel Barenboim  (standard complete set)
Ingrid Haebler  (standard complete set)
Friedrich Wührer  (complete set)
Dieter Zechlin  (complete set)

*We are here not far away from the sound world of Schubert's near-contemporaries Carl Maria von Weber and Felix Mendelssohn-Bartholdy. Haebler brings out delightful contrasts between the four movements of this little performed work: it might be described as "middle-period" from this tragically short creative life-span*

4/Individual Sonatas/continued
**Sonata in F sharp minor  D571/D604/D570/**
*composed around July 1817*

Allegro moderato
Klavierstück
Scherzo-Allegro vivace
Allegro

*Versions auditioned*
Paul Badura-Skoda  (complete set)
Martino Tirimo  (complete set)

*These are the only two pianists to offer this reconstruction  (from three different sources) with its rhapsodic first movement.  The Klavierstück D604,  inserted by Badura-Skoda as a second movement,  can be heard elsewhere as a separate entity in recorded performances by Kempff and Richter*

4/Individual Sonatas/continued

**Sonata in D  D575**/*composed around August 1817*
Allegro ma non troppo
Andante
Scherzo-Allegretto
Allegro giusto

*Versions auditioned*
Alfred Brendel  (standard complete set)
Michael Endres (complete set)
Ingrid Haebler  (standard complete set)
Sviatoslav Richter  (versions in Florence,  Aldeburgh, Tokyo,  London and Moscow)
Friedrich Wührer  (complete set)
Dieter Zechlin  (complete set)

*An ambitious work which progresses from an opening of Beethoven-like grandeur to passionate yearning (second movement) and a joyous dance finale which looks forward to the one in the late Sonata D958. Richter's hypersensitive and detailed response is rivalled only by the "Viennese" contingent Wührer and Haebler.  However,  neither would I want to be without Zechlin's buoyant traversal.*

4/Individual Sonatas/continued

**Sonata in C D613/D612**/*composed around April 1818*
Moderato
Adagio
Allegretto

*Version auditioned*
Paul Badura-Skoda (complete set)

*It may be questionable whether this reconstruction, with movements in turn florid, devotional and volatile, really deserves to be included in the canon of Schubert's Sonatas*

4/Individual Sonatas/continued

**Sonata in F minor D625**/*composed around September 1818*
Allegro
Scherzo-Allegretto
Allegro

*Versions auditioned*
Paul Badura-Skoda (complete set)
Wilhelm Kempff (standard complete set)
Sviatoslav Richter (versions in Munich, Tokyo, London and Moscow)
Friedrich Wührer (complete set)
Dieter Zechlin (complete set)

*This unfinished piece is offered in various stages of completion, either with the final movement ending abruptly as in Schubet's manuscript or, in the case of Badura-Skoda and Richter, with the addition of the Adagio D505.*

*The work is in turn assertive or tender in mood: typically for the composer, questions are asked but answers not always delivered. I would describe it as the first mature Schubert sonata, whose manic undertones are fully relished by Richter.*

4/Individual Sonatas/continued
**Sonata in A D664**/composed around 1818
Allegro moderato
Andante
Allegro

*Versions auditioned*
Claudio Arrau  (Philips  432 3072)
Ingrid Haebler  (standard complete set)
Myra Hess  (Appian APR 7504)
Radu Lupu  (standard complete set)
Eldar Nebolsin  (Naxos  8.572459)
Sviatoslav Richter  (versions in Paris,  Munich,  Tokyo, London and Moscow)

*Formal perfection may not have been a top priority for Schubert in his sonatas,  yet he comes close to it here: a serene opening movement with turbulent interjections, a haunting lullaby for second movement and a dance-like conclusion which gradually increases in buoyancy.*

*The 1928 American Columbia recording by Dame Myra Hess is certainly one of the first ever of a complete Schubert sonata, easily predating the 1930s sessions by Schnabel.  Strangely on its CD reissue by Appian, the reviewer criticises the interpretation for a certain "Victorian, old-fashioned sentiment",  an assessment with which I do not agree.*

*I have not been able to trace a copy of a late recording of the piece by the veteran Lili Kraus for the American Vanguard label,  which could be of great interest.*

4/*Individual Sonatas/continued*
**Sonata in A minor  D784**/composed around February 1823
Allegro giusto
Andante
Allegro vivace

*Versions auditioned*
Paul Badura-Skoda  (complete set)
Daniel Barenboim  (standard complete set)
Imogen Cooper  (Avie  AV 2158)
Paolo Giacometti  (Channel Classics  CCS 10697)
Emil Gilels  (Sony  88751 77312)
Lili Kraus  (Warner Erato  2564 242328)
Elisabeth Leonskaya  (Easonus  EAS 29300)
Paul Lewis  (set of Late Sonatas)
Sviatoslav Richter  (versions in Tokyo, London & Moscow)
Hans Richter-Haaser  (Warner Classics  993 7252)
Friedrich Wührer  (complete set)
Dieter Zechlin  (complete set)

*4/Individual Sonatas/Sonata in A minor D784/continued*

*If the term "sepulchral" can be applied to a piece of music, here is a case in point: the lone figure in swirling mists in a Caspar David Friedrich painting is evoked in this sonata, with harsh contrasts between piano and forte. There is little consolation to be found in the breathtakingly beautiful Lieder-like melodies, as they are dispelled by those jagged cascades of notes so typical of the composer when his mind is under pressure.*

*Lewis and Richter are the most successful in presenting this tortured soundscape, showing no fear in extending the tempo when called for: by contrast, Kraus and Richter-Haaser (recorded twenty-seven years apart in the same Abbey Road venue) offer more conventional and urbane readings. Gilels offers a finely poised account in his New York recording, not deserving the dismissive comments about his Schubert playing by the critic in a recent edition of Radio 3's "CD Review". Giacometti competes with Badura-Skoda by offering a version of the Sonata for pianoforte.*

4/Individual Sonatas/continued
**Sonata in C "Reliquie" D840**/*composed around April 1825*
Moderato
Andante

*Versions auditioned*
Paul Badura-Skoda (1968 and complete set)
Imogen Cooper (Avie AV 2158)
Wilhelm Kempff (complete set)
Paul Lewis (set of Late Sonatas)
Gerhard Oppitz (complete set)
Sviatoslav Richter (versions in Paris, Moscow & Leverkusen)
Rudolf Serkin (Sony 88750 515629)
Friedrich Wührer (complete set)

*The opening movement of this Sonata is a forerunner in its breadth to the corresponding one in D960, seeming to pose a question to which various possible answers are then tried out: the bittersweet themes gain from being taken at the moderate tempo indicated – or perhaps even a shade slower (Richter and Oppitz).*

*The strong performance by Serkin is only marred by the harsh recorded sound so typical of CBS in the mono LP era.*

*A second movement Andante, with its variations on a Lied-like theme, completes the satisfying torso which Schubert left us (two further movements are played by Richter and Kempff in their incomplete form). However, there are also interesting arguments for the reconstructions, marked Presto and Allegro, played by Badura-Skoda and Wührer (the latter in a completion attributed to the Austrian composer Ernst Krenek).*

4/Individual Sonatas/continued
**Sonata in A minor D845**/*composed around May 1825*
Moderato
Andante poco mosso
Allegro vivace-Trio
Allegro vivace

*Versions auditioned*
Daniel Barenboim (complete set)
Alfred Brendel (complete set)
Imogen Cooper (Avie AV 2156)
Michael Endres (complete set)
Ingrid Haebler (complete set)
Clara Haskil (Music and Arts CD 542)
Wilhelm Kempff (1953 and complete set)
Lili Kraus (Warner Erato 2564 624223)
Elisabeth Leonskaya (Easonus EAS 29300)
Radu Lupu (complete set)
Gerhard Oppitz (complete set)
Maria Joao Pires (Deutsche Grammophon 477 8107)
Sviatoslav Richter (profil medien PH 17005)
Andras Schiff (complete set)
Friedrich Wührer (complete set)
Christian Zacharias (complete set)
Dieter Zechlin (complete set)

## 4/Individual Sonatas/Sonata in A minor D845/continued

*On the surface this work, described on its first publication as "Grande Sonate", exudes more optimisim and confidence than some of its immediate predecessors. However, by observing every repeat and holding back on tempi, Sviatoslav Richter (in his Melodiya studio recording from 1957) is virtually alone in revealing the doubts and insecurities which were obviously haunting the composer by the mid 1820s.*

*The strange march-like feel to the opening movement, with its concluding hammered-out coda, suggests nothing less than a dance of death. A second movement with sparkling variations lifts the spirits somewhat, but by the end of its 10-minute span has only revealed more uncertainty. The menacing third movement does have a lighter trio section but leads on to a frantic finale.*

4/*Individual Sonatas/continued*
**Sonata in D  D850**/*composed around August 1825*
Allegro
Con moto
Allegro vivace-Trio
Allegro moderato

*Versions auditioned*
Leif Ove Andsnes  (EMI 516 4482)
Imogen Cooper  (Avie  AV 2156)
Clifford Curzon  (Decca)
Emil Gilels  (Sony  88751 77312)
Elisabeth Leonskaya  (Easonus 29300)
Paul Lewis  (live and studio versions)
Sviatoslav Richter  (versions in Prague and Moscow)
Artur Schnabel  (Music and Arts CD 1173)
Friedrich Wührer  (complete set)

*4/Individual Sonatas/Sonata in D  D850/continued*

*After the turbulent cascades of a comparatively brief Allegro vivace comes an extended Adagio con moto of real solace:  its themes's first leisurely statement is followed by a repeat with variations to provide one of those heart-stopping moments of which Schubert was past master.  At the risking of sounding repetitious,  I have to say that it is only Richter who fully relishes such  "heavenly lengths" and who also fully realises the finale's buoyant lilt -  perhaps most successfully in his Prague concert recording from 1956.  Leonskaya also comes close - she was after all an associate of Richter – not to mention Lewis in his 2011 Wigmore Hall concert recording.*

*This is the point in our survey of the Sonatas when the name of Schnabel enters the field with a pioneering recording made for HMV in 1936.  However,  on the showing of this particular work,  I would not place the versions of Schnabel,  or that of his coeval Curzon,  at the top of the list.*

4/Individual Sonatas/continued
**Sonata in G D894**/*composed around October 1826*
Molto moderato e cantabile
Andante
Allegro moderato-Trio
Allegretto

*Versions auditioned*
Claudio Arrau  (Philips  432 3072)
Paul Badura-Skoda  (complete set)
Daniel Barenboim  (complete set)
Alfred Brendel  (complete set)
Imogen Cooper  (Avie  AV 2157)
Michael Endres  (complete set)
Eduard Erdmann  (Tahra TAH 218-219)
David Fray  (Warner Erato 461 6699)
Ingrid Haebler  (complete set)
Wilhelm Kempff  (complete set)
Radu Lupu  (complete set)
Gerhard Oppitz  (complete set)
Sviatoslav Richter  (versions in Moscow and London)
Arcadi Volodos  (Sony SK 89647)
Friedrich Wührer  (complete set)
Dieter Zechlin  (complete set)

*Another bleak landscape is evoked when Schubert's spacious first movement is played with sufficient breadth. Playing times for this movement in the versions listed above vary from 9'31" (Wührer) to a surprising 26'57" (Richter in London): between these extremes fall a host of moderate options (Badura-Skoda, Barenboim, Endres, Haebler, Lupu). Many interpreters start with the "molto moderato e cantabile" indicated, but then gradually accelerate in the course of the development. The result of this is a mood more of nostalgia than despair, which may of course fit better in the comfort zone of some listeners. There are hammer blows at the end of that first movement, but I do admit that they are gentle ones.*

*The positive third movement anticipates the Scherzo and Trio in the Great C Major Symphony D944, and leads to a finale of real happiness (strikingly realised in the Bayerischer Rundfunk recording by Erdmann).*

*My personal preference goes to Richter (no surprise there!), Fray and Volodos.*

4/Individual Sonatas/continued
**Sonata in C minor  D958**/*composed around September 1828*
Allegro
Adagio
Menuetto-Allegro
Allegro

*Versions auditioned*
Leif Ove Andsnes  (EMI 516 4482)
Claudio Arrau  (Philips  432 3072)
Paul Badura-Skoda  (complete set)
Daniel Barenboim  (complete set)
Alfred Brendel  (complete set)
Imogen Cooper  (BBC Proms & Avie  AV 2157)
Youri Egorov  (Etcetera  KTC 1469)
Michael Endres  (complete set)
Eduard Erdmann  (Tahra TAH 218-219)
Ingrid Haebler  (complete set)
Wilhelm Kempff  (complete set)
Sebastian Knauer  (Berlin Classics BC 11902)
Elisabeth Leonskaya  (Easonus EAS 29300)
Paul Lewis  (Harmonia mundi HMA 195 1755)
Nikolai Lugansky  (2015 concert recording)
Radu Lupu  (complete set)
Gerhard Oppitz  (complete set)
Maurizio Pollini  (Deutsche Grammophon  419 2292)
Sviatoslav Richter  (versions in Budapest,  Salzburg & Moscow)
Hans Richter-Haaser  (Warner Classics 993 7252)
Friedrich Wührer  (complete set)
Christian Zacharias  (complete set)
Dieter Zechlin  (complete set)

*4/Individual Sonatas/Sonata in C minor D958/continued*

*An opening movement of more conciseness and rhythmic vitality than is usual with Schubert – a year earlier he had been a pallbearer at Beethoven's funeral and perhaps here strove to pay his tribute.  In the Adagio we are communing direct with Schubert's melodic gift in one of its most concentrated expressions,  with sublime variations on its prime theme,  and then the calmest of conclusions.  After the briefest of minuets we are thrown with abandon into a joyous dance finale, again recalling that in D944.*

*The younger generation of performers (Knauer, Andsnes,  Lewis) seem to excel in this less introvert of the sonatas,  but I still turn to the older players (Badura-Skoda,  Erdmann,  Richter)  for those special insights.*

4/*Individual Sonatas/continued*
**Sonata in A D959**/*composed around September 1828*
Allegro
Andantino
Scherzo
Rondo

*Versions auditioned*
Claudio Arrau  (Philips  432 3072)
Daniel Barenboim  (complete set)
Imogen Cooper  (Avie  AV 2156)
Eduard Erdmann  (2 versions - Tahra TAH 218-219 & TAH 386-387)
Christoph Eschenbach  (Brilliant Classics 9189)
Ingrid Haebler  (complete set)
Wilhelm Kempff  (complete set)
Lili Kraus  (FNAC 642 328)
Elisabeth Leonskaya  (Easonus 29300)
Paul Lewis  (Harmonia Mundi HMC 901800)
Francesco Piemontesi  (BBC Music Magazine)
Maurizio Pollini  (Deutsche Grammophon  419 2292)
Andras Schiff  (complete set)
Artur Schnabel  (Music and Arts CD 1173)
Rudolf Serkin  (Sony 88750 515629)
Mitsuko Uchida  (BBC recording)
Friedrich Wührer  (complete set)
Dieter Zechlin  (complete set)

4/Individual Sonatas/Sonata in A  D959/continued

A pivotal moment in the entire Schubert Sonata oeuvre comes in this work's Andantino:  after a poignant opening we are suddenly faced with what Paul Badura-Skoda describes as an "apocalyptic vision of destruction and death which is similar in spirit to the rectitative "Und der Vorhang im Tempel zerriss" from Bach's Matthew Passion".  The best interpreters of this sonata are to my mind those who allow something of the unease of that frightening moment to permeate,  albeit imperceptibly, the comparative serenity of the outer movements (Schnabel,  Erdmann,  Serkin, Eschenbach, Kraus, Lewis, Piemontesi, Uchida, Zechlin – Kraus,  in particular, achieves it with remarkably brisk tempi).

4/Individual Sonatas/continued
**Sonata in B Flat D960**/*composed around September 1828*
Molto moderato
Andante sostenuto
Allegro vivace con delicatezza
Allegro ma non troppo

*Versions auditioned*
Adrian Aeschbacher  (Deutsche Grammophon  LPM 18 139)
Geza Anda  (Deutsche Grammophon LPM 18 880/SLPM 138 880)
Leif Ove Andsnes  (EMI 516 4482)
Claudio Arrau  (Philips  432 3072)
Paul Badura-Skoda  (complete set)
Daniel Barenboim  (complete set)
Alfred Brendel  (complete set)
Imogen Cooper  (Avie  AV 2158)
Clifford Curzon  (Decca 074 3186)
Michael Endres  (complete set)
Eduard Erdmann  (3 versions – 1944,  1950 and 1952)
Christoph Eschenbach  (Brilliant Classics 9189)
Leon Fleisher  (United Archives UAR 021)
Anthony Goldstone  (Divine Art 2-1202)
Ingrid Haebler  (complete set)
Clara Haskil  (Philips  442 6852)
Vladmir Horowitz  (Deutsche Grammophon  474 3702)
Cyprien Katsaris  (Piano P21-042A)
Wilhelm Kempff  (complete set and 1950 version)
Lili Kraus  (Vanguard  08 407071)
Elisabeth Leonskaya  (Easonus 29300)
Paul Lewis  (Harmonia mundi HMC 901 800)
Gerhard Oppitz  (complete set)
Maria Joao Pires  (Deutsche Grammophon 477 8107)
Maurizio Pollini  (Deusche Grammophon 419 2292)

4/Individual sonatas/Sonata in B Flat  D960/concluded
*Versions auditioned/continued*
Sviatoslav Richter (versions in Aldeburgh, Salzburg, Prague & Moscow)
Artur Schnabel  (Music and Arts CD 1175)
Rudolf Serkin  (Sony 88750 515629 – contains 2 versions)
Mitsiko Uchida  (BBC concert recording)
Friedrich Wührer  (complete set)
Dieter Zechlin  (complete set)

*And so we reach the finale of the rewarding journey through these twenty sonatas, crowned by this one in B flat.  To quote Paul Badura-Skoda again, the last sonata "expresses the dignity and detachment with which a man confronts his final moments". With thematic material recalling the Lieder "Am Meer" and "Der Wanderer", we are carried on a journey from which there seems to be no return.  Such a state of mind was encountered once before in the opening of D894, and as I did then I think it worthwhile to note the extreme variations in playing time for that first movement: from 12'05" (Erdmann) to a full 25'00" (Richter).  The interpreter is called upon, it seems to me, to adopt the broadest of tempi, even when (as in so many of the earlier recordings) repeats are eschewed.  As for the second movement, it is "a lament which takes us beyond pain" (Badura-Skoda again).*

*Apart from Richter, I hear interpretations of considerable stature from Endres, Eschenbach, Fleisher, Lewis, Oppitz, Pires and Serkin.*

## 5/FANTASY, IMPROMPTUS, MOMENTS MUSICAUX, KLAVIERSTUECKE AND OTHER SOLO PIECES

**Fantasy in C D760 "Wanderer"**/*composed around November 1822*
Allegro con fuoco ma non troppo-
Adagio-
Presto-
Allegro

*Versions auditioned*
Paul Badura-Skoda (Gramola 99031)
Alfred Brendel (Decca 480 1218)
Clifford Curzon (Philips 456 7572)
Edwin Fischer (Appian APR 5515)
Anthony Goldstone (Divine Art 2-1202)
Wilhelm Kempff (Deutsche Grammophon 453 2892)
Lili Kraus (Vanguard 08 407071)
Eldar Nebolsin (Naxos 8.572459)
Elly Ney (2 versions - Piano Library PL 329 & Colosseum 9025)
Gerhard Oppitz (Hänssler 98 616)
Sviatoslav Richter (2 versions - EMI 217 4112 & Profil Medien PH 17005)

*Before the comparatively recent re-assessment of the Sonatas, this Fantasy seems to have been the most popular of Schubert's larger scale keyboard works, with pioneering recorded versions from Fischer (1934), Ney (1941) and Curzon (1949) - it is the last of these that impresses most with fine contrasts of mood. Among more recent offerings, the ones that strike me most are those by Richter, Nebolsin and Oppitz.*

*As an afterthought, be warned that if you sample Fischer's version, you might just find his bold and wilful approach irresistible!*

5/Fantasy, Impromptus, Moments musicaux,
Klavierstücke and other pieces/continued

**Moments musicaux D780**/*composed around 1823-1824*
No 1 in C (Moderato)
No 2 in A flat (Andantino)
No 3 in F minor (Allegro moderato)
No 4 in C sharp minor (Moderato)
No 5 in F minor (Allegro vivace)
No 6 in A flat (Allegretto)

*Versions auditioned (only complete sets included)*
Adrian Aeschbacher (Deutsche Grammophon LPE 17 090)
Claudio Arrau (EMI 918 4322)
Joerg Demus (DG LPEM 19 159/SLPEM 136 007)
Anthony Goldstone (Divine Art 2-1202)
Friedrich Gulda (Scribendum SC 016)
Ingrid Haebler (Decca 478 5859)
Radu Lupu (Decca)
Gerhard Oppitz (Hänssler 98 298)
Rudolf Serkin (Sony 88750 515629)
Artur Schnabel (Music and Arts CD 1175)
Dieter Zechlin (Berlin Classics BC 018 44828)

*Might these concise gems perhaps be considered as studies for sonata movements? Their freshness and insouciance certainly looks forward to the "Kinderszenen" of Robert Schumann, whilst there are also echoes of Schubert's own "Rosamunde" incidental music (and not just in the well-known Allegro moderato).*

*Arrau, Haebler and Zechlin are my preferred choices, although I cannot fault any of the other versions.*

*5/Fantasy, Impromptus, Moments musicaux,
Klavierstücke and other pieces/continued*
**Impromptus D899**/*composed around 1827*
No 1 in C minor  (Allegro molto moderato)
No 2 in E flat  (Allegro)
No 3 in G  (Andante)
No 4 in A flat  (Allegretto)

*Versions auditioned  (only complete sets included)*
Daniel Barenboim  (Deutsche Grammophon  415 8492)
Clifford Curzon  (Philips 456 7572)
Joerg Demus  (DG  LPEM 19 159/SLPEM 136 007)
Edwin Fischer  (Appian APR 5512)
Robert Goldsand  (Concert Hall  CHS 1146)
Friedrich Gulda  (Scribendum  SC 016)
Ingrid Haebler  (2 versions – Vox STPL 58940 & Philips 478 5859)
Sebastian Knauer  (Berlin Classics  BC 11902)
Gerhard Oppitz  (Hänssler Classics  98 521)
Maria Joao Pires  (Deutsche Grammophon  457 5502)
Artur Schnabel  (Music and Arts  CD 1175)

*The first piece in this set evokes another desolate landscape, where moments of heartbreaking beauty raise our hopes, only to be dashed by a return to despair.  The other three pieces are altogether lighter in character,  which is perhaps the reason why they have remained some of Schubert's most popular melodies.*

*Pires endows that expansive first Impromptu with great poignancy,  although the less sophisticated approach of Schnabel or Curzon in the complete set has its own merit.*

5/Fantasy, Impromptus, Moments musicaux,
Klavierstücke and other pieces/continued
**Impromptus D935**/composed December 1827
No 1 in F minor (Allegro moderato)
No 2 in A flat (Allegretto)
No 3 in B flat Andante (Tema con variazioni)
No 4 in F minor (Allegro scherzando)

*Versions auditioned (only complete sets included)*
Daniel Barenboim (Deutsche Grammophon 415 8492)
Clifford Curzon (Philips 456 7572)
Joerg Demus (DG LPEM 19 160/SLPEM 136 008)
Edwin Fischer (Appian APR 5512)
Robert Goldsand (Concert Hall CHS 1146)
Anthony Goldstone (Divine Art 2-1202)
Ingrid Haebler (2 versions – Vox STPL 58940 & Decca 478 5859)
Sebastian Knauer (Berlin Classics BC 16182)
Lili Kraus (Vanguard OVC 8200)
Gerhard Oppitz (Hänssler Classics 98 519)
Maria Joao Pires (Deutsche Grammophon 457 5502)
Artur Schnabel (Music and Arts CD 1175)

*This group bears more coherence as a set than D899, and Robert Schumann apparently considered it a sonata in all but name. I hear a journey which never truly reaches its goal, in which happiness is always viewed through a veil of tears.*

*Amongst modern interpreters Pires stands out, and perhaps the clear recorded sound helps, along with tempi which are considerably more expansive than those of the pioneers Fischer, Schnabel and Curzon.*

5/Fantasy, Impromptus, Moments musicaux,
Klavierstücke and other pieces/continued
**Klavierstücke D946**/composed around May 1828
Allegro assai – Andante
Allegretto
Allegro

*Versions auditioned*
Claudio Arrau (EMI 918 4322)
Alfred Brendel (Decca 480 1218)
Imogen Cooper (Avie AV 2156)
Joerg Demus (DG LPEM 19 160/SLPEM 136 008)
Wilhelm Kempff (Deutsche Grammophon 453 2892)
Paul Lewis (Harmonia mundi HMC 902 115-116)
Gerhard Oppitz (Hänssler Classics 98 287)
Maria Joao Pires (Deutsche Grammophon 457 5502)
Sviatoslav Richter (Profil Medien PH 17005)

*I first got to know this fascinating tryptich through the poised
and urbane recording by Kempff, and later that of Arrau,
but deeper insights can be encountered in the readings
of later generations of pianists (Lewis, Oppitz, Pires)
with tempi which on the whole are much broader.*

*There is sunlight to be found in the three pieces, albeit
tinged with that characteristic Schubertian melancholy;
the middle section of the Allegretto forms a climax
of the most urgent yearning.*

*5/Fantasy, Impromptus, Moments musicaux, Klavierstücke and other pieces/continued*
**Klavierstück in A  D604**/*composed around 1816-1817*

*Versions auditioned*
Eileen Joyce  (Appian  APR 7502)
Wilhelm Kempff  (Deutsche Grammophon  453 2892)
Gerhard Oppitz  (Hänssler Classics  98 569)
Sviatoslav Richter  (Versions in Aldeburgh and Moscow)

*This is the free-standing piece used by Badura-Skoda to complete the Sonata in F Sharp minor  (see page 73)*


**Allegretto in C minor  D915**/*composed around April 1827*

*Versions auditioned*
Claudio Arrau  (EMI  918 4322)
Alfred Brendel  (Decca  480 1218)
Anthony Goldstone  (Divine Art  2-1202)
Wilhelm Kempff  (Deutsche Grammophon  453 2892)
Sebastian Knauer  (Berlin Classics  BC 11902)
Elisabeth Leonskaya  (BBC Concert recording)
Gerhard Oppitz  (Hänssler Classics  98 521)
Sviatoslav Richter  (Versions in Paris,  Aldeburgh, Florence and Moscow)
Andras Schiff  (Decca  478 3018)
Artur Schnabel  (Music and Arts  CD 1173)

*Contemplative and expansive,  this piece fully deserves its place in the remarkable body of the late keyboard music which culminated in the last three Sonatas.*

*5/Fantasy, Impromptus, Moments musicaux, Klavierstücke and other pieces/continued*
**Adagio in G  D178**/*composed around April 1815*
**Adagio in E  D612**/*composed around April 1818*

*Version auditioned*
Gerhard Oppitz  (Hänssler Classics  98 569)

*D612 also used by Badura-Skoda to reconstruct the Sonata in C (see page 75)*

**Adagio in D Flat  D505**/*composed around September 1818*

*Version auditioned*
Gerhard Oppitz  (Hänssler Classics  98 617)

**Andante in C  D29**/*composed around September 1812*

*Version auditioned*
Gerhard Oppitz  (Hänssler Classics  98 569)

*5/Fantasy, Impromptus, Moments musicaux, Klavierstücke and other pieces/continued*
**Fantasy in C minor D2e**/*composed around 1811*

*Version auditioned*
Gerhard Oppitz (Hänssler Classics 98 570)


**Fantasy in C D605a "Grazer"**/*composed around 1818*

*Version auditioned*
Lili Kraus (Columbia Odyssey 3216 0380)


**March in E D606**/*composed around 1818*

*Versions auditioned*
Claudio Arrau (EMI 918 4322)
Sviatoslav Richter (Melodiya MELCD 10 02231-02234)
Artur Schnabel (Music and Arts CD 1173)


**Rondo in E D506**/*composed around June 1817*

*Version auditioned*
Gerhard Oppitz (Hänssler Classics 98 618)

*Also used by Badura-Skoda and Richter to complete the Sonata in E minor D566 (see page 71)*

*5/Fantasy, Impromptus, Moments musicaux, Klavierstücke and other pieces/continued*
**Scherzo in D  D570**/*composed around July 1817*

*Version auditioned*
Gerhard Oppitz  (Hänssler Classics 98 570)


**2 Scherzi  D593**/*composed around November 1817*
No 1 in B
No 2 in D Flat

*Versions auditioned*
Paolo Bordoni  (Divox CDX 25251)
Nikolai Lugansky  (2015 concert recording)
Radu Lupu  (Decca)
Gerhard Oppitz  (Hänssler Classics 98 519)


**Ungarische Melodie in B minor  D817**/
*composed around September 1824*

*Versions auditioned*
Alfred Brendel  (Decca 480 1218)
David Fray  (Warner Erato 461 6699)
Sebastian Knauer  (Berlin Classics BC 11902)
Gerhard Oppitz  (Hänssler Classics 98 617)
Artur Schnabel  (Music and Arts CD 1173)

*5/Fantasy, Impromptus, Moments musicaux, Klavierstücke and other pieces/concluded*
**10 Variations in F  D156**/*composed around February 1815*

*Version auditioned*
Gerhard Oppitz  (Hänssler Classics 98 617)


**13 Variations on a theme by Hüttenbrenner  D576/**
*composed around August 1817*

*Versions auditioned*
Wilhelm Kempff  (Deutsche Grammophon 453 2892)
Gerhard Oppitz  (Hänssler Classics 98 616)
Sviatoslav Richter  (AS-Disc  AS 325)


**Variation on a waltz by Diabelli  D718**/*composed around March 1821*

*Versions auditioned*
Paolo Bordoni  (Divox CDX 25251)
Michael Endres  (Capriccio  C 7125)
Gerhard Oppitz  (Hänssler Classics 98 616)

## FRANZ SCHUBERT: THE DANCE MUSIC FOR SOLO KEYBOARD

### 6/COMPLETE OR NEAR COMPLETE SET
(77 Deutsche Tänze, 28 Minuets, 92 Waltzes, 58 Ecossaises, 40 Ländler, 1 Trio and 1 Cotillon)

**Michael Endres**
D2d, D41, D91, D128, D139, D145, D146, D158,
D299, D335, D354, D365, D366, D378, D380,
D421, D511, D529, D600, D610, D643, D679,
D680, D681, D697, D722, D734, D735, D769,
D779, D781, D782, D783, D790, D816, D820,
D841, D924, D925, D969, D970, D971, D973,
D974, D975, D976, D977, D978, D979

CD: Capriccio C 7125
*Recorded in Cologne WDR Funkhaus between December 1993-July 1997*

*This valuable set, which also embraces 17 of the Sonatas, seems to offer the solo dance music in an edition as near complete as current scholarship permits. It is repertoire which has so far received only modest scrutiny in the recording studios*

# FRANZ SCHUBERT: THE DANCE MUSIC FOR SOLO KEYBOARD

## 7/INDIVIDUAL SETS OF DANCES

**Wiener Deutsche Tänze D128**/*composed around 1812*

*Versions auditioned*
Paolo Bordoni  (Divox  CDX 25251)
Michael Endres  (complete set)


**17 Deutsche Tänze (Ländler) D366/**
*composed around July-November 1824*

*Versions auditioned*
Paolo Bordoni  (Divox  CDX 25251)
Michael Endres  (complete set)
Lili Kraus  (Columbia Odyssey  3216 0380)
Sviatoslav Richter (Selections in Aldeburgh, Paris & Moscow)


**6 Ecossaises D421**/*composed around 1816*

*Versions auditioned*
Michael Endres  (complete set)
Sviatoslav Richter  (Selection in Moscow)

7/Individual sets of solo dance music/continued
**Minuet in C sharp minor D600**/*composed around 1814*

*Versions auditioned*
Paolo Bordoni  (Divox  CDX 25251)
Michael Endres  (complete set)


**34 Valses sentimentales  D779**/*composed around 1825*

*Versions auditioned*
Paolo Bordoni  (EMI 1C057 18211)
Michael Endres  (complete set)
Lili Kraus  (Selection on FNAC 642 328)

*Many of these Valses became popular in the transcriptions by Franz Liszt under the title "Soirees de Vienne"*


**11 Ecossaises  D781**/*composed around January 1823*

*Versions auditioned*
Paolo Bordoni  (Divox  CDX 25251)
Alfred Brendel  (Decca  480 1218)
Michael Endres  (complete set)

7/*Individual sets of solo dance music/continued*
**16 Deutsche Tänze with 2 Ecossaises  D783**/
*composed around 1823-1825*

*Versions auditioned*
Paolo Bordoni  (Divox  CDX 25251)
Alfred Brendel  (Decca 480 1218)
Michael Endres  (complete set)


**12 Deutsche Tänze  D790**/*composed around May 1823*

*Versions auditioned*
Paolo Bordoni  (Divox  CDX 25251)
Alfred Brendel  (Decca 480 1218)
Michael Endres  (complete set)
Leon Fleisher  (United Archives UAR 021)


**Grazer Galopp  D925**/*composed around September 1827*

*Versions auditioned*
Michael Endres  (complete set)
Lili Kraus  (Columbia Odyssey  3216 0380)

*7/Individual sets of solo dance music/concluded*
**12 Valses nobles D969**

*Versions auditioned*
Paolo Bordoni (EMI 1C057 18211)
Michael Endres (complete set)


**2 Deutsche Tänze D974**

*Versions auditioned*
Michael Endres (complete set)
Lili Kraus (Columbia Odyssey 3216 0380)

## 8/FRANZ SCHUBERT: THE KEYBOARD MUSIC FOR 4 HANDS

**Variations on an original theme  D603**

*Versions auditioned*
Anthony Goldstone & Caroline Clemmow  (Olympia OCD 672)
Ingrid Haebler & Ludwig Hoffmann  (Decca 478 5859)
Lili Kraus & Homero de Magalhaes  (Warner Erato 2564 242328)


**Rondo in D  D608**/*composed around January 1818*

*Versions auditioned*
Paul Badura-Skoda & Joerg Demus  (Nixa WLP 5047)
Ingrid Haebler & Ludwig Hoffmann  (Decca 478 5859)


*To any listener sampling Schubert's output for piano duet for the first time,  either of the above-listed items would provide an ideal introduction.  Such works,  composed for the convivial atmosphere of a friends' gathering,  convey a happiness and relaxation such as is found much more rarely in the solo music  (least of all in the sonatas)*

*8/Keyboard music for 4 hands/continued*
**3 Marches militaries  D733**/*composed around 1818*
No 1 in D  (Allegro vivace)
No 2 in G  (Allegro molto moderato)
No 3 in E Flat  (Allegro moderato)

*Versions auditioned*
Christoph Eschenbach & Justus Frantz  (EMI  569 7642)
Anthony Goldstone & Caroline Clemmow  (Olympia OCD 673)
Artur Schnabel & Karl Ulrich Schnabel  (Music and Arts CD 1173)

*The first of these Marches has of course achieved even wider popularity in an orchestral transcription*


**Grand Duo in C  D812/**composed around June 1824
Allegro moderato
Andante
Allegro vivace
Allegro vivace

*Versions auditioned*
Paul Badura-Skoda & Joerg Demus  (Nixa  WLP 5047)
Imogen Cooper & Paul Lewis  (BBC Proms recording)
Christoph Eschenbach & Justus Frantz  (EMI  569 7702)
Anthony Goldstone & Caroline Clemmow  (Olympia OCD 671)
Sviatoslav Richter & Benjamin Britten  (Decca  478 6778)

*8/Keyboard music for 4 hands/continued*
**Variations in A Flat on an original theme  D813/**
*composed around May-July 1824*

*Versions auditioned*
Anthony Goldstone & Caroline Clemmow  (Olympia OCD 674)
Paul Lewis & Steven Osborne  (Hyperion  CDA 67665)
Sviatoslav Richter & Benjamin Britten  (Decca  478 6778)
Andreas Staier & Alexander Melnikov (Harmonia mundi HMM 902227)

*This delightful set of variations emerges as almost a*
*masterpiece in the hands of the master pianists*
*Richter and Britten.  Staier and Melnikov may be*
*the first duo to offer the work on fortepiano.*


**Divertissement a la hongroise in G minor  D818/**
*composed around 1824*
Andante
Marcia – Trio
Allegretto

*Versions auditioned*
Christoph Eschenbach & Justus Frantz  (EMI  569 7702)
Anthony Goldstone & Caroline Clemmow  (Olympia  OCD 673)
Alfons & Alois Kontarsky  (DG  LPE 17 200/SLPE 133 012)
Lili Kraus & Homero de Magalhaes  (Warner Erato  2564 242328)
Artur Schnabel & Karl Ulrich Schnabel  (Music and Arts  CD 1173)

*Conceived during one of two stays in the Hungarian*
*region of Zseliz, Schubert skilfully merges his own*
*characteristic keyboard style with a distinctive*
*local flavour in this test piece for the two*
*daughters of Count Esterhazy.  How they coped*
*with the highly flamboyant third movement is*
*not recorded!*

8/Keyboard music for 4 hands/continued
**6 Grandes marches et trios  D819/**
*composed between 1818-1824*
No 1 in E Flat  (Allegro maestoso)
No 2 in G minor  (Allegro ma non troppo)
No 3 in B minor  (Allegretto)
No 4 in D  (Allegro maestoso)
No 5 in E Flat minor  (Andante)
No 6 in E  (Allegro con brio)

*Version auditioned*
Christoph Eschenbach & Justus Frantz  (EMI  569 7642)

*The recorded set of the 4-hand piano music by Eschenbach and Frantz would be worth acquiring for the sake of this performance alone:  this grand collection of large-scale marches with a total playing time of around 55 minutes, must surely rank as a major compositional achievement in its category,  indeed in Schubert's entire piano oeuvre. Teeming with variety and joie de vivre,  notwithstanding occasional moments of introspection  (the fifth movement andante does give way to a familiar Schubertian melancholy),  the marches straddle the composer's middle and late periods and are brought to vivid life in the hands of Eschenbach and Frantz.*

8/Keyboard music for 4 hands/continued

**Divertissement a la francais in E minor  D823/**
*composed around 1826-1827*
Tempo di marcia
Andantino varie
Rondeau brillant

*Version auditioned*
Christoph Eschenbach and Justus Frantz  (EMI  569 7702)

*This finely balanced full-scale divertissement, in every way the equal to D818, fell victim to the ambitions of a publisher who decided to issue the three sections as separate works: thus losing the thematic relations and leading to a tradition of playing the second part (Andantino varie) as an independent piece. Sadly both the Artur Schnabel-Karl Ulrich Schnabl and Sviatoslav Richter-Benjamin Britten duos do this (albeit with playing of considerable delicacy).*


**2 Marches caracteristiques in C  D886**

*Versions auditioned*
Paul Badura-Skoda & Joerg Demus  (2 versions – Nixa & DG)
Christoph Eschenbach & Justus Frantz  (EMI  569 7642)
Anthony Goldstone & Caroline Clemmow  (Olympia  OCD 675)
Ingrid Haebler & Ludwig Hoffmann  (Decca 478 5859)

*Brightly extrovert in character, both these pieces have more reflective middle sections whose contrast is most effectively brought out by the Viennese duo of Haebler and Hoffmann*

*8/Keyboard music for 4 hands/continued*
**Fantasy in F minor D940**/*composed around January-April 1828*
Allegro molto moderato-
Largo-
Allegro vivace

*Versions auditioned*
Paul Badura-Skoda & Joerg Demus  (2 versions – Nixa & DG)
Christoph Eschenbach & Justus Frantz  (EMI  569 7702)
David Fray & Jacques Rouvier  (Warner Erato  461 6699)
Anthony Goldstone & Caroline Clemmow  (Olympia  OCD 672)
Ingrid Haebler & Ludwig Hoffmann  (Decca  478 5859)
Paul Lewis & Steven Osborne  (Hyperion  CDA 67665)
Radu Lupu & Murray Perahia  (Sony  88697 858112)
Sviatoslav Richter & Benjamin Britten  (Decca  458 6778)
Andreas Staier & Alexander Melnikov (Harmonia mundi HMM 902227)

*Staier and Melnikov may be the first duo to offer*
*the work on fortepiano*

*8/Keyboard music for 4 hands/continued*
**Allegro in A minor  D947  "Lebensstürme"/**
*composed around May 1828*

*Versions auditioned*
Christoph Eschenbach & Justus Frantz  (EMI  569 7702)
David Fray & Jacques Rouvier  (Warner Erato  461 6699)
Paul Lewis & Steven Osborne  (Hyperion  CDA 67665)
Artur Schnabel & Karl Ulrich Schnabel  (Music and Arts CD 1173)

*It is the Schnabel duo which to my ears most successfully captures this fascinating piece with a second subject of the utmost poignancy:  here is music which is indeed beyond sadness.*

8/Keyboard music for 4 hands/continued
**Grand rondeau in A D951**/*composed around June 1828*
Allegretto quasi Andantino

*Versions auditioned*
Martha Argerich & Daniel Barenboim  (BBC Proms recording)
Martha Argerich & Nelson Freire  (Deutsche Grammophon 477 8570)
Paul Badura-Skoda & Joerg Demus  (2 versions – Nixa & DG)
Christoph Eschenbach & Justus Frantz  (EMI  569 7642)
Anthony Goldstone & Caroline Clemmow  (Olympia  OCD 673)
Paul Lewis & Steven Osborne  (Hyperion  CDA 67665)
Artur Schnabel & Karl Ulrich Schnabel  (Music and Arts CD 1173)
Andreas Staier & Alexander Melnikov (Harmonia mundi HMM 902227)

*Chronologically this is the final major piece for piano duet*
*which Schubert composed,  and it is not difficult to detect*
*a sense of farewell to a medium which obviously brought*
*him such satisfaction.  Again it is the Schnabels who,*
*with their pioneering recording from October 1937,*
*offer the perfect combination of dexterity and*
*warm  resignation.*

*8/Keyboard music for 4 hands/continued*
**3 Marches heroiques  D602**/*composed between 1818-1824*
No 1 in B minor  (Allegro moderato)
No 2 in C  (Maestoso)
No 3 in D  (Moderato)

**Deutscher Tanz in G minor  D618**/*composed around 1818*

**Grande marche funebre in C minor  D859**/
*composed around December 1825*

**Grande marche heroique in A minor  D885**/
*composed around 1825-1826*

**Kindermarsch in G minor  D928**/*composed around October 1827*


*Version of these works auditioned*
Christoph Eschenbach & Justus Frantz  (EMI  569  7642)

8/Keyboard music for 4 hands/concluded
**Fantasy in G  D1**/*composed around April-May 1810*
**Fantasy in G  D9**/*composed around September 1811*
**Fantasy in C  D48**/*composed around April-June 1813*
**4 Polonaises  D599**/*composed around July 1818*
**Sonata in B  D617**/*composed around 1818*
**Variations on a French song  D624/**
*composed around September 1818*
**Overture in G  D668**/*composed around October 1819*
**Overture in F  D675**/*composed around November 1819*
**4 Ländler  D814**/*composed around July 1824*
**6 Polonaises  D824**/*composed between April-July 1826*
**Variations on a theme from Herold's *Marie*  D908/**
*composed around 1827*
**Fugue in E  D952**/*composed around June 1828*
**Allegro and Andante  D968**

*Apart from a Naxos series employing a variety of pianist duos, these least-known compositions may only have been recorded in the edition by the duo Goldstone-Clemmow, which has proved difficult to trace in its entirety on the Olympia label. However, following the death of Anthony Goldstone early in 2017, there are apparently plans to re-issue that complete set of the 4-hand piano music on the Divine Art label: this will fill a significant gap in the Schubert catalogue.*

## 9/SVIATOSLAV RICHTER/THE SCHUBERT DISCOGRAPHY

This is updated from my 1999 discography *Pianist of the Century* and gives fullest possible details (recording dates, recording locations and issue numbers) of Richter's significant contribution to Schubert on record.

It will be quite clear that Richter's recorded Schubert legacy is not to be overlooked when any comparisons are made. Those who, like me, are attuned to the Russian pianist's close affinity with Franz Schubert's darker side, will only regret that he did not take more of the piano works into his working repertoire: as with most other composers, Richter was highly selective in his choice of repertoire and stubbornly refused, with very few exceptions, to cultivate the pursuance of completeness so beloved of the major record companies in the glory days of the long-playing record. As far as Schubert is concerned, our main regret must be that we therefore have no complete sets from Richter of such masterworks as the *Impromptus* or *Moments musicaux*.

On the other hand we do have Richter's contribution to a couple of chamber works as well as the *Lieder* recordings with his wife Nina Dorliak, the tenor Peter Schreier and baritone Dietrich Fischer-Dieskau.

*9/Richter Schubert discography/continued*
**Sonata in E minor  D566**

*Concert recording in Moscow on 5 February 1958*
cd:  profil medien  PH 17005
*original 2-movement version*

*Concert recording in Moscow on 29 November 1962*
cd:  profil medien  PH 17005

*Concert recording in Aldeburgh Parish Church on 20 June 1964*
lp:  rococo records  2121
cd:  as-disc AS 325/historical performers  HPS 10/ music and arts  CD 642/bbc legends  BBCL 41462

*Televised concert in Aldeburgh Snape Maltings Concert Hall on 27 September 1977*
Unpublished video recording

*Concert recording in Moscow Grand Hall of the Conservatoire on 2 May 1978*
cd:  melodiya  MELCD 10 02231

*Concert recording in Munich on 23 July 1978*
cd:  melodiya (japan)  VICC 60077

*Concert recording in Moscow Grand Hall of the Conservatoire on 18 October 1978*
cd:  melodiya  MELCD 10 02231

9/Richter Schubert discography/continued
**Sonata in D  D575**

*Concert recording in Moscow on 12 October 1965*
cd:  brilliant classics  92229-92233

*Concert recording in Firenze on 12 June 1966*
cd:  philips  438 4832/442 4642/decca 478 6778
*438 4832 and 442 4642 were incorrectly described as a 1979 recording in Hohenems*

*Concert recording in Aldeburgh Jubilee Hall on 21 June 1966*
lp:  penzance records  PR 22
cd:  music and arts CD 600

*Concert recording in Tokyo Koseinenkin Hall between 7-24 February 1979*
lp:  victor (japan)  VIC 28012/eurodisc  203 728.425/
chant du monde  LDX 78726-78727/emi SLS 5289/
1C157 65040-65041/ricordi  ARCL 227003/
melodiya  C10 15309-15310
cd:  eurodisc  880 013.231/olympia  OCD 286/OCD 5012

*Concert recording in London Royal Festival Hall on 31 March 1979*
cd:  bbc  WMCU 00102/bbc legends  BBCL 40102

*Concert recording in Moscow Grand Hall of the Conservatoire on 8 June 1979*
cd:  brilliant classics  92229-92233/
melodiya  MELCD 10 02231

9/Richter Schubert discography/continued
**Sonata in F minor  D625**

*Concert recording in Munich on 23 July 1978*
cd: melodiya (japan)  VICC 60076

*Concert recording in Moscow Grand Hall of the Conservatoire on 18 October 1978*
cd: melodiya  MELCD 10 02231

*Concert recording in Tokyo Koseinenkin Hall between 7-24 February 1979*
lp: victor (japan)  VIC 28012/eurodisc  203 728.425/
chant du monde  LDX 78726-78727/emi  SLS 5289/
1C157 65040-65041/ricordi  ARCL 227003/
melodiya  C10 15309-15310
cd: eurodisc  880 013.231/olympia  OCD 286/OCD 5012

*Concert recording in London Royal Festival Hall on 31 March 1979*
cd:  bbc  WMCU 00102/bbc legends  BBCL 40102

9/Richter Schubert discography/continued
**Sonata in A  D664**

*Concert recording in Kiev on 27 June 1957*
cd:  profil medien   PH 17005

*HMV recording in Paris Salle Wagram between*
*11 February-11 April 1963*
lp:  ALP 2011/FALP 788/QALP 10379/ASD 561/ASDF 788/
CVL 788/CVB 1788/electrola E 80692/SME 80692/
angel  36150/32078/emi  SXLP 30297/1C063 00299/
2C069 00299/3C065 00299
cd:  emi  764 4292/767 1972/217 4112/warner
classics  9029 593016/profil medien  PH 17005

*Concert recording in Munich on 23 July 1978*
cd:  melodiya  (japan)   VICC 60077

*Concert recording in Moscow Grand Hall of the*
*Conservatoire on 18 October 1978*
cd:  melodiya   MELCD 10 02231

*Concert recording in Tokyo Koseinenkin Hall*
*between 1-7 February 1979*
lp:  victor (japan)  VIC 28007/eurodisc  203 476.425/
chant du monde  LDX 78726-78727/emi  SLS 5289/
1C157 65040-65041/ricordi  ARCL 227003/melodiya
C10 15349-15340/vox  C 9027/DVCL 9027
cd:  eurodisc  880 011.231/olympia  OCD 288/OCD 5012

*Concert recording in London Royal Festival Hall*
*on 31 March 1979*
cd:  bbc  WMCU 00102/bbc legends  BBCL 40102

9/Richter Schubert discography/continued
**Sonata in A minor  D784**

*Concert recording in Moscow on 8 April 1957*
cd:  profil medien  PH 17005

*Concert recording in Tokyo Koseininkin Hall*
*between 1-7 February 1979*
lp: victor (japan)  VIC 28007/eurodisc  203 476.425/
chant du monde  LDX 78726-78727/emi  SLS 5289/
1C157 65040-65041/ricordi  ARCL 227003/
vox C 9027/DVCL 9027/melodiya  C10 15349-15350
cd:  eurodisc  880 011.231/olympia  OCD 288/OCD 5012

*Concert recording in London Royal Festival Hall*
*on 31 March 1979*
cd:  bbc  WMCU 00112


**Sonata in C "Reliquie"  D840**

*Chant du Monde recording in Paris on 19-20 October 1961*
lp:  LDX 8295/LDX 7943/LDXS 78295/concert hall  CM 2251/
hall of fame  HOF 528/HOFS 528/monitor  MC 2057/MCS 2057/
melodiya  D 011755-011756/M10 11755 007
cd:  monitor  55.008/MCD 72057/profil medien  PH 17005

*Concert recording in Moscow on 13 November 1961*
cd: profil medien  PH 17005

*Concert recordings in Salzburg on 27 November 1979 and*
*Leverkusen on 17 December 1979*
cd:  philips  416 2922/416 2892/438 4832/442 4642/
decca  478 6778
*This recording appears to be a montage from the 2 concerts*

*9/Richter Schubert discography/continued*
**Sonata in A minor D845**

*Melodiya recording in Moscow on 2 March 1957*
lp: melodiya  D 04594-04595/M10 04594 004/
mk records  MK 5002/DO 4594/eurodisc  XAK 86041/
204 374.250/monitor  MC 2027/MCS 2027/
parlophone  PMA 1049
cd: monitor  55.012/rca-bmg  GD 69050/74321 294632/
74321 294602/istituto discografico italiano  IDIS 6584/
profil medien  PH 17005
*incorrectly described by profil medien as a concert recording*


**Sonata in D D850**

*Concert recording in Prague Rudolfinum on 14 June 1956*
cd:  praga  PR 25 4031/CMX 354001

*Melodiya recording in Moscow on 11 August 1956*
lp: melodiya  D 03638-03639/mk records  DO 3638/
monitor  MC 2043/MCS 2043
cd: rca-bmg  74321 294632/74321 294602/
profil medien  PH 17005
*incorrectly described by profil medien as a concert recording*

*9/Richter Schubert discography/continued*
**Sonata in G D894**

*Televised concert in Aldeburgh Snape Maltings
Concert Hall on 27 September 1977*
Unpublished video recording
*Extensive extract from the recording can be seen on
Warner Music Vision 3984 230292 (Richter: The Enigma)*

*Concert recording in Moscow Grand Hall of the
Conservatoire on 2 May 1978*
cd:  brilliant classics 92229-92233/melodiya MELCD 10 02231

*Concert recording in London Royal Festival Hall on
20 March 1989*
cd:  philips  438 4832/442 4642/decca  478 6778

*9/Richter Schubert discography/continued*
**Sonata in C minor  D958**

*Concert recording in Moscow on 5 February 1958*
cd:  profil medien  PH 17005

*Radio recording in Budapest on 9 February 1958*
lp:  longanesi  GCL 26
cd:  as-disc  AS 325/notes  PGP 11011/memories  HR 4436-4437/ historical performers  HPS 10/music and arts  CD 957/ istituto discografico italiano  IDIS 6584

*Concert recording in Moscow Grand Hall of the Conservatoire on 6 October 1971*
cd:  melodiya  MELCD 10 02231

*Eurodisc recording in Salzburg Schloss Klessheim on 12 August 1972*
lp:  MK 85792/chant du monde  LDX 7943/LDS 78560/ melodiya  CM 04177-04178/C10 04177 001/angel  40254/ columbia (usa)  M 35151/quintessence  PMC 7208
cd:  880 091.231/rca-bmg  GD 69050/olympia  OCD 335/ OCD 5012/sony music  88875 199912

*9/Richter Schubert discography/continued*
**Sonata in B Flat  D960**

*Concert recording in Moscow on 9 May 1957*
cd:  preiser  95003/profil medien  PH 17005

*Concert recording in Moscow on 13 November 1961*
cd:  brilliant classics  92229-92233/profil medien  PH 17005

*Concert recording in Aldeburgh Parish Church on
20 June 1964*
cd:  music and arts  CD 642/bbc legends  BBCL 41462

*Concert recording in Prague Rudolfinum on
24 September 1972*
cd:  praga  PR 254032/CMX 354001

*Eurodisc recording in Salzburg Schloss Anif on
6-9 November 1972*
lp:  MK 86222/chant du monde  LDX 7943/emi  SLS 890/
melodiya  CM 04187-04188/C10 04187 008
cd:  880 092.250/olympia  OCD 335/OCD 5012/
sony music  88875 199912

9/Richter Schubert discography/continued
**Wanderer Fantasy D760**

*Concert recording in Moscow on 29 November 1962*
cd: profil medien  PH 17005

*Concert recording in London Royal Festival Hall*
*on 2 February 1963*
cd: bbc legends  BBCL 41462

*HMV recording in Paris Salle Wagram between*
*11 february-11 april 1963*
lp: ALP 2011/FALP 788/QALP 10379/ASD 561/ASDF 788/
electrola  E 80692/SME 80692/angel  36150/emi  SXLP 30297/
1C063 00299/2C069 00299/3C065 00929
cd: emi  566 9472/572 5672/572 5792/747 9672/764 4292/
767 1972/217 4112/warner classics  9029 593016/
profil medien  PH 17005


**Impromptu in G Flat  D899 No 3**

*Concert recording in Moscow on 19 February 1957*
cd: profil medien  PH 17005

*Concert recording in Kiev on 12 June 1959*
cd: profil medien  PH 17005

*Concert recording in Moscow Grand Hall of the*
*Conservatoire on 18 October 1978*
cd: melodiya  MELCD 10 02231

9/Richter Schubert discography/continued
**Impromptu in E Flat D899 No 2**

*Melodiya recording in Moscow in 1950*
78: CCCP 021051-021052
lp: D 00369-00370/D 4594-4595/D 011777-011778/eurodisc XAK 86041/mk records MK 5002/DO 4594/hall of fame HOF 525/HOFS 525/monitor MC 2027/MCS 2027
cd: monitor 55.012/MCD 72057/naxos 8.111352

*Concert recording in Moscow on 19 February 1957*
cd: profil medien PH 17005

*Concert recording in Sofia on 25 February 1958*
45: philips ABE 10211/SBF 249
lp: philips ABL 3301/A00584L/GL 5677/6768 219/ 6780 502/columbia (usa) ML 5396
cd: philips 420 7742/454 1662/454 1672/456 9462/ decca 478 6778

*Concert recording in Moscow Grand Hall of the Conservatoire on 3 May 1978*
cd: melodram MELCD 10 02231

*Concert recording in Tokyo Koseinenkin Hall between 1-24 February 1979*
lp: victor (japan) VIC 28047/eurodisc 204 005.425/ emi SLS 5289/1C157 65040-65041/ricordi OCL 16203/ melodiya C10 16399 002
cd: olympia OCD 288/OCD 5012

*9/Richter Schubert discography/continued*
**Impromptu in A Flat D899 No 4**

*Concert recording in Sofia on 25 February 1958*
45: philips ABE 10212
lp: philips ABL 3301/A00584L/6768 219/6780 052/
columbia (usa) ML 5396
cd: philips 420 7742/454 1662/454 1672/456 9462/
decca 478 6778

*Concert recording in Kiev on 12 June 1959*
cd: profil medien PH 17005

*Concert recording in New York Carnegie Hall on 19 October 1960*
lp: sony (japan) SONC 15066
cd: sony music 88430 147207

*Concert recording in Dubrovnik on 14 August 1967*
lp: croatia records K 5069393

*Concert recording in Prague Rudolfinum on 24 September 1972*
cd: praga PR 254032/CMX 354001

*Concert recording in Moscow Grand Hall of the Conservatoire on 3 May 1978*
cd: melodiya MELCD 10 02231

*Concert recording in Munich on 23 July 1978*
cd: melodiya (japan) VICC 60077

*Concert recording in Tokyo Konseinenkin Hall between 1-24 February 1979*
lp: victor (japan) VIC 28047/eurodisc 204 005.425/
ricordi OCL 16203/emi SLS 5289/1C157 65040-65041/
melodiya C10 16399 002
cd: olympia OCD 288/OCD 5012

9/Richter Schubert discography/continued
**Impromptu in A Flat  D935 No 2**

*Melodiya recording in Moscow in 1952*
78:  D 00369-00370
lp:  D 04594-04595/D 011777-011778/CM 04165-04166/
M10 04594 004/C10 04165 000/eurodisc  ZK 78347/
XAK 86041/XAK 87474/204 374.250/columbia (usa)
M 33826/hall of fame  HOF 525/HOFS 525/mk records
MK 5002/DO 4594/monitor  MC 2027/MCS 2027
cd:  monitor  55.012/MCD 72057/rca-bmg  GD 69050/
74321 294652/74321 294602/naxos  8.111352

*Chant du monde recording in Paris on 19-20 October 1961*
cd:  profil medien  PH 17005
*this recording was not included on the original lp*

*Eurodisc recording in Salzburg Schloss Klessheim
on 26 September 1971*
lp:  MK 85792/XB 25296/chant du monde  LDX 7943/
LDX 78560/melodiya  CM 04177-04178/C10 04177 001/
angel  40254/quintessence  PMC 7208
cd:  880 091.231/sony music  88875 199912

9/Richter Schubert discography/continued
**Moment musical in C D780 No 1**

*Melodiya recording in Moscow in 1952*
78: CCCP 20857-20858
lp: D 019217-019218/CM 04165-04166/C10 04165 000/
eurodisc XAK 87474/columbia (usa) M 33826
cd: rca-bmg 74321 294652/74321 294602/naxos 8.111352

*Concert recording in Moscow on 19 February 1957*
cd: profil medien PH 17005

*Concert recording in Sofia on 25 February 1958*
45: philips ABE 10212
lp: philips ABL 3301/A00584L/6768 219/6780 502/
columbia (usa) ML 5396
cd: philips 420 7742/454 1662/454 1672/456 9462/
decca 478 6778

*Concert recording in Aldeburgh Jubilee Hall on 22 June 1965*
cd: bbc legends BBCL 41462

*Concert recording in Moscow Grand Hall of the Conservatoire on 2 May 1978*
cd: melodiya MELCD 10 02231

*Concert recording in Munich on 23 July 1978*
cd: melodiya (japan) VICC 60077

*Concert recording in Tokyo Konseinenkin Hall on 13 February 1979*
lp: victor (japan) VIC 28047/eurodisc 204 005.425/
emi SLS 5289/1C157 65040-65041/ricordi OCL 16203/
melodiya C10 16399-16310/C10 16399 002
cd: olympia OCD 286/OCD 5012

9/Richter Schubert discography/continued
**Moment musical in F minor   D780 No 3**

*Melodiya recording in Moscow in 1950*
lp:  D 019217-019218/CM 04165-04166/C10 04165 000/
eurodisc  XAK 87474/columbia (usa)  M 33826
cd:  rca-bmg  74321 294652/74321 294602

*Concert recording in Moscow on 19 February 1957*
cd:  profil medien  PH 17005

*Chant du monde recording in Paris on 19-20 October 1961*
lp:  LDX 8295/LDX 7943/LDXS 78295/concert hall CM 2251/
hall of fame  HOF 528/HOFS 528/melodiya
D 011755-011756/M10 11755 007
cd:  profil medien  PH 17005

*Concert recording in Aldeburgh Jubilee Hall on 22 June 1965*
cd:  bbc legends  BBCL 41462

*Concert recording in Moscow Grand Hall of the*
*Conservatoire on 2 May 1978*
cd:  melodiya  MELCD 10 02231

*Concert recording in Munich on 23 July 1978*
cd:  melodiya (japan)  VICC 60077

*Concert recording in Tokyo Konseinenkin Hall on*
*13 February 1979*
lp:  victor (japan)  VIC 28047/eurodisc  204 005.425/
emi  SLS 5289/1C157 65040-65041/ricordi  OCL 16203/
melodiya  C10 16399-16400/C10 16399 002
cd:  olympia  OCD 286/OCD 5012

*9/Richter Schubert discography/continued*
**Moment musical in A Flat   D780 No 6**

*Melodiya recording in Moscow in 1950*
lp:  D 019217-019218/CM 04165-04166/C10 01465 000/
eurodisc  XAK 87474/columbia (usa)  M 33826
cd:  rca-bmg 74321 294652/74321 294602

*Concert recording in Moscow on 19 February 1957*
cd:  profil medien  PH 17005

*Concert recording in Aldeburgh Jubilee Hall on 22 June 1965*
lp:  rococo  2121
cd:  music and arts  CD 722/bbc legends  BBCL 41462

*Concert recording in Moscow Grand Hall of the Conservatoire on 2 May 1978*
cd:  melodiya  MELCD 10 02231

*Concert recording in Tokyo Konseinenkin Hall on 13 February 1979*
lp: victor (japan)  VIC 28047/eurodisc  204 005.425/
emi  SLS 5289/1C157 65040-65041/ricordi  OCL 16203/
melodiya  C10 16399-16400/C10 16399 002
cd:  olympia  OCD 286/OCD 5012

*9/Richter Schubert discography/continued*

**3 Klavierstücke  D946**
*Concert recording in Budapest on 27 April 1963*
cd:  profil medien  PH 17005

**Klavierstück  D946 No 1  (original version)**
*Concert recording in Moscow on 13 November 1961*
cd:  profil medien  PH 17005

**Allegretto in C minor  D915**
*Chant du monde recording in Paris on 19-20 October 1961*
lp:  LDX 8295/LDX 7943/LDXS 78295/concert hall  CM 2251/
hall of fame  HOF 528/HOFS 528/monitor MC 2057/MCS 2057/
melodiya  D 011755-011756/M10 11755 007
cd:  profil medien  PH 17005

*Concert recording in Moscow on 13 November 1961*
cd:  profil medien  PH 17005

*Concert recording in Firenze on 23 October 1962*
lp:  deutsche grammophon  LPM 18 950/SLPM 138 950/
2548 286
cd:  deutsche grammophon  447 3552/447 4202/457 6672/
decca  478 6778

*Concert recording in Moscow in Grand Hall of the
Conservatoire on 2 May 1978*
cd:  melodiya  MELCD 10 02231

9/Richter Schubert discography/continued
**Klavierstück in A  D604;  Scherzo in D Flat  D593**

*Televised concert in Aldeburgh Snape Maltings
Concert Hall on 27 September 1977*
lp:  columbia (usa)  M3-35197/cbs  79316
cd:  sony music  88843 014702
*Video recording remains unpublished*

*Concert recording in Moscow Grand Hall of the
Conservatoire on 2 May 1978*
cd:  melodiya  MELCD 10 02231


**March in E  D606**
*Concert recording in Moscow Grand Hall of the
Conservatoire on 3 May 1978*
cd:  melodiya  MELCD 10 02231


**Variations on a theme by Hüttenbrenner  D576**
*Concert recording in Manchester on 8 October 1969*
cd:  as-disc  AS 325/historical performers  HP 10/
bbc  WMCU 00112


**12 Waltzes from D145**
*Concert recording in Moscow on 19 February 1957*
cd:  profil medien  PH 17005

9/Richter Schubert discography/continued
**Deutsche Tänze from D790**  (in the order 8-11-8);
**Ecossaises from D421**  (in the order 1-3-1-2-1-6);
**Ecossaises from D734**  (in the order 1-2-3-1)

*Concert recording in Moscow on 19 February 1957*
cd: profil medien  PH 17005 (D734 only)

*Concert recording in Moscow Grand Hall of the Conservatoire on 18 October 1978*
cd: melodiya  MELCD 10 02231


**Ländler from D366**  (in the order 1-3-5-4-5-4-1)

*Concert recording in Moscow on 19 February 1957*
cd: profil medien  PH 17005

*Chant du monde recording in Paris on 19-20 October 1961*
lp: LDX 8295/LDX 7943/LDXS 78295/concert hall CM 2251/hall of fame  HOF 528/HOFS 528/monitor  MC 2057/MCS 2057/melodiya  D 011755-011756/M10 11755 007
cd: profil medien  PH 17005

*Concert recording in Firenze on 23 October 1962*
lp: deutsche grammophon  LPM 18 950/SLPM 138 950/2548 286
cd: deusche grammophon  447 3552/447 4202/457 6672/decca  478 6778

*Televised concert in Aldeburgh Snape Maltings Concert Hall on 27 September 1977*
lp: columbia (usa)  M3-35197/cbs  79316
cd: sony music  88843 014702
*Video recording remains unpublished*

*Concert recording in Moscow Grand Hall of the Conservatoire on 2 May 1978*
cd: melodiya  MELCD 10 02231

*9/Richter Schubert discography/continued*
**Grand Duo in C for piano 4 hands D812; Variations on an original theme for piano 4 hands D813**
with Benjamin Britten, piano

*Concert recordings in Aldeburgh Jubilee Hall on 22 June 1965 (D812) and Aldeburgh Parish Church on 20 June 1964 (D813)*
lp: rococo 2121
cd: as-disc AS 328/music and arts CD 721 (D812)/ CD 722 (D813)/decca 478 6778/profil medien PH 17005 (D813)


**Andantino varie (Divertissement a la francais) for piano 4 hands D823**
with Benjamin Britten, piano

*Concert recording in Aldeburgh Jubilee Hall on 22 June 1965*
lp: rococo 2121
cd: music and arts CD 722/decca 478 6778


**Fantasy in F minor for piano 4 hands D940**
with Benjamin Britten, piano

*Concert recording in Aldeburgh Jubilee Hall on 22 June 1965*
lp: rococo 2121
cd: as-disc AS 328/music and arts CD 722/ decca 478 6778

*9/Richter Schubert discography/continued*
**Violin Sonata in A  D574**

*Concert recording in Tours Grand Theatre on 2 July 1967*
with David Oistrakh, violin
lp: rococo  2097

*Concert recording in Paris on 4 December 1968*
with David Oistrakh, violin
cd: chant du monde  LDC 278 855

*Concert recording in Moscow on 7 December 1985*
with Oleg Kagaan, violin
cd: live classics  LCL 172


**Piano Quintet in A  D667  "Die Forelle"**
*Concert recording in Schloss Hohenems on 18 June 1980*
with members of Borodin String Quartet and
Georg Hörtnagel, double-bass
lp: emi  ASD 4032/1C063 43041/2C069 43041/
3C065 43041/angel 37846
cd: emi  572 5672/572 5792/747 0092/217 4112/
warner classics  9029 593016


**Erlkönig, in the piano transcription by Liszt**
*Concert recording in Moscow on 8 December 1949*
cd: profil medien  PH 17005

*9/Richter Schubert discography/continued*
**Winterreise, Lied-Zyklus D911**
with Peter Schreier, tenor

*Eterna recording in Dresden Lukaskirche on 17 February 1985*
lp: 827 992/philips 416 1941
cd: philips 416 2892/442 3602/decca 478 6778

*Televised concert in Moscow Pushkin Museum on*
*10 December 1985*
lp: melodiya C10 00289 006
*Video recording remains unpublished*


**Die Post/Winterreise**
(Von der Strasse her ein Posthorn klingt)
with Nina Dorliak, soprano (in Russian)
*Melodiya recording in Moscow on 19 December 1953*
lp: D 026457-026458
cd: cascavelle VEL 3041/profil medien PH 17005


**Die Krähe/Winterreise**
(Eine Krähe war mit mir aus der Stadt gezogen)
with Nina Dorliak, soprano (in Russian)
*Melodiya recording in Moscow in 1956*
lp: D 009307-009308/D 026457-026458
cd: cascavelle VEL 3041/profil medien PH 17005

*9/Richter Schubert discography/continued*
**Die Taubenpost/Schwanengesang D957**
(Ich hab' eine Brieftaub' in meinem Sold);
**Lied der Mignon D877/Goethe-Lieder**
(Nur wer die Sehnsucht kennt)
with Nina Dorliak, soprano (in Russian)
*Melodiya recording in Moscow in 1956*
lp: D 009307-009308/D 026457-026458
cd: cascavelle VEL 3041/profil medien PH 17005


**Sei mir gegrüsst D741** (O du Entriss'ne mir)
with Nina Dorliak, soprano (in Russian)
*Melodiya recording in Moscow on 19 September 1953*
lp: D 026457-026458/M10 46751 001
cd: cascavelle VEL 3041/profil medien PH 17005

9/Richter Schubert discography/continued
**Abschied/Schwanengesang D957**
(Ade du muntre du fröhliche Stadt!)

with Nina Dorliak, soprano (in Russian)
*Melodiya recording in Moscow on 19 September 1953*
lp: M10 46751 001
cd: cascavelle VEL 3041/profil medien PH 17005

with Dietrich Fischer-Dieskau, baritone
*Concert recording in Salzburg Kleines Festspielhaus on 29 August 1977*
cd: orfeo C334 931B/C339 930T


**Die Vögel D691** (Wie lieblich und fröhlich)
**Nachtviolen D752** (Nachtviolen, Nachtviolen)
**Der Einsame D800** (Wann meine Grillen schwillen)
**Geheimes D719** (Ueber meines Liebchens Aeugeln)
**Nacht und Träume D827** (Heil'ge Nacht, du sinkest nieder)
with Dietrich Fischer-Dieskau, baritone
*Concert recording in Salzburg Kleines Festspielhaus on 27 August 1977*
cd: orfeo C334 931B/C339 930T

*9/Richter Schubert discography/continued*
**Die Sterne D939** (Wie blitzen die Sterne)
**Fischerweise D881** (Den Fischer fechten Sorgen)
**Auf der Donau D553** (Auf der Wellen Spiegel)
**Am Fenster D878** (Ihr lieben Mauern hold und traut)
**Des Fräuleins Liebeslauschen D698** (Da unten steht ein Ritter)
**Der Wanderer D649** (Wie deutlich des Mondes Licht)
**Auf der Bruck D853** (Frisch trabe sonder Ruh und Rast)
**Im Frühling D882** (Still sitz' ich an des Hügels Hang)
with Dietrich Fischer-Dieskau, baritone

*Concert recording in Tours Grand Theatre on 2-4 July 1977*
lp: deutsche grammophon  2530 988
cd: deutsche grammophon  423 0552/445 7172/
decca 478 6778

*Concert recording in Salzburg Grosses Festspielhaus on 29 August 1977*
cd: orfeo  C334 931B/C339 930T

*Televised concert in Schloss Ismaning in September 1978*
dvd included with the cd-set  477 5556 (dietrich
fischer-dieskau: an die musik)

*9/Richter Schubert discography/concluded*
**Versunken D715** (Voll Locken kraus ein Haupt so rund)
with Dietrich Fischer-Dieskau, baritone

*Concert recording in Salzburg Kleines Festspielhaus on*
*27 August 1977*
cd: orfeo C334 931B/C339 930T

*Televised concert in Schloss Ismaning in September 1978*
dvd included with the cd-set 477 5556 (dietrich
fischer-dieskau: an die musik)


**Aus Heliopolis D754** (Fels auf Felsen hingewälzet)
**Des Sängers Habe D832** (Schlagt mein ganzes Glück in Splitter)
**Wehmut D772** (Wenn ich durch Wald und Fluren geh')
**Der Strom D565** (Mein Leben waltz sich murrend fort)
**Das Zügenglöckchen D871** (Kling die Nacht durch, klinge!)
**Abendbilder D650** (Still beginnt's im Hain zu tauen)
**Der Schiffer D536** (Im Winde, im Sturme)
**Totengräbers Heimweh D842** (O Menschheit, o Leben, was soll's?)
with Dietrich Fischer-Dieskau, baritone

*Concert recording in Tours Grand Theatre on 2-4 July 1977*
lp: deutsche grammophon 2539 988
cd: deutsche grammophon 423 0552/445 7172/decca 478 6778

*Concert recording in Salzburg Kleines Festspielhaus on*
*27 August 1977*
cd: orfeo C334 931B/C 339 930T

## 10/ARTUR SCHNABEL/THE SCHUBERT DISCOGRAPHY

As was the case with Richter, this is also a revision of the Schubert section of my earlier Schnabel discography, which appeared in the volume *Giants of the Keyboard*. And as we are concerned here with recordings made during the shellac era (to be precise, between 1932-1950), I have now added the matrix numbers: these appear in the left-hand column, to the right of which can be found the original 78rpm catalogue numbers.

Also in common with Richter, I have added the Schubert chamber and *Lieder* recordings in which Schnabel participated (his partner in the group of *Lieder* was his wife, the contralto Therese Behr-Schnabel).

There is not really any need to emphasise again the importance of Artur Schnabel's pioneering work for Franz Schubert's keyboard output, not just in these early Abbey Road recordings for the HMV label, but also in his public performances: sadly only a handful of fragmentary recordings of the latter seem to have survived.

*10/Schnabel Schubert discography/continued*
**Sonata in B  D575:  Allegretto from bar 77 to end**

*Concert recording in New York Town Hall on 11 January 1942*
lp:  MJA records  MJA 1966


**Sonata in A  D664:  Incomplete performance**

*Concert recording in New York Town Hall on 4 January 1942*
Unpublished radio broadcast
*Sections of the music are missing in all four movements*


**Sonata in A minor  D845:  Allegro vivace**

*US Armed Forces recording in New York City in 1944*
lp:  armed forces radio services/discocorp  BWS 724

*10/Schnabel Schubert discography*
**Sonata in D  D850**

*HMV recording in London Abbey Road No 3 Studio on 26-27 January 1939*
2EA 7438    DB 3756/victor M 888
2EA 7439
2EA 7440    DB 3757/victor M 888
2EA 7441
2EA 7442    DB 3758/victor M 888
2EA 7443
2EA 7444    DB 3759/victor M 888
2EA 7445
2EA 7446    DB 3760/victor M 888
lp:  COLH 83/toshiba  GR 2052/emi  1C147 01557-01558M/ 3C153 01220-01222/RLS 7713/EX 29 07883/ arabesque AR 8137
cd:  arabesque  Z 6573/emi  764 2592/ music and arts  CD 1173

10/Schnabel Schubert discography/continued
**Sonata in A  D959**

*HMV recording in London Abbey Road No 3 Studio on 14-15 January 1937*
2EA 4543    DB 3103/DB 21418/victor M 580
2EA 4544
2EA 4545    DB 3104/DB 21419/victor M 580
2EA 4546
2EA 4547    DB 3105/DB 21420/victor M 580
2EA 4548
2EA 4549    DB 3106/DB 21421/victor M 580
2EA 4550
2EA 4551    DB 3107/DB 21422/victor M 580
lp: COLH 84/emi  1C147 01557-01558M/RLS 143 5603/ EX 29 07883/arabesque  AR 8143
cd: arabesque  Z 6571/emi  764 2592/regis  1415/ music and arts  CD 1173
*78rpm edition was also published in automatic coupling with the catalogue numbers DB 8322-8326 and DB 9733-9737*

*10/Schnabel Schubert discography/continued*
**Sonata in B Flat D960**

*HMV recording in London Abbey Road Studio No 3
on 25-26 January 1939*
2EA 7428     DB 3751/DB 21353
2EA 7429
2EA 7430     DB 3752/DB 21354
2EA 7431
2EA 7432     DB 3753/DB 21355
2EA 7433
2EA 7434     DB 3754/DB 21356
2EA 7435
2EA 7436     DB 3755/DB 21357
lp: COLH 33/emi 1C147 01557-01558M/3C153 01220-01222/
RLS 143 5603/EX 29 07883/arabesque AR 8145
cd: arabesque Z 6575/emi 764 2592/regis 1415/
warner classics 265 0642/music and arts CD 1173
*78rpm edition was also published in automatic coupling with
the catalogue numbers DB 8826-8830 and DB 9700-9704*

*10/Schnabel Schubert discography/continued*
**Impromptu in C minor   D899 No 1**

*RCA Victor recording in New York City RCA Victor Studios on 18 and 23 June 1942*
075293      unpublished
075294
cd: sony music  88985 389712

*HMV recording in London Abbey Road Studio No 1 on 6 June 1950*
2EA 14755   DB 21320
2EA 14756
45: victor  WHMV 1027
lp: BLP 1007/FALP 295/victor  LHMV 1027/LCT 1019/ electrola  E 80684/toshiba  GR 2083/emi  1C047 01339M/ 2C051 01339/RLS 7713/arabesque  AR 8137
cd: arabesque  Z 6592/emi  586 8332/warner classics  265 0642/music and arts  CD 1173

10/Schnabel Schubert discography/continued
**Impromptu in E Flat  D899 No 2;**
**Impromptu in G Flat  D899 No 3**

*RCA Victor recording in New York City RCA Victor Studios on 18 and 23 June 1942*
075295     unpublished
075296
cd: sony music  88985 389712

*HMV recording in London Abbey Road Studio No 3 on 7 June 1950*
2EA 14757   DB 21355
2EA 14758
45: victor  WHMV 1027
lp: BLP 1007/FALP 295/HQM 1142/victor LHMV 1027/LCT 1019/electrola  E 80684/ toshiba  GR 2083/seraphim  60115/emi 1C047 01339M/2C051 01339/RLS 7713/ arabesque  AR 8137
cd: arabesque  Z 6592/emi  586 8332/warner classics  265 0642/music and arts  CD 1173

*10/Schnabel Schubert discography/continued*
**Impromptu in A Flat D899 No 4**

*Welte-Mignon piano roll recorded in Freiburg in May 1905*
Roll number 383
cd: tacet 146

*RCA Victor recording in New York City RCA Victor Studios on 18 and 23 June 1942*
075297      unpublished
075298
cd: sony music  88985 389712

*HMV recording in London Abbey Road Studio No 3 on 7-8 June 1950*
2EA 14759   DB 21351
2EA 14760
45: victor  WHMV 1027
lp: BLP 1007/FALP 295/HQM 1142/victor  LHMV 1027/ LCT 1019/electrola  E 80684/toshiba  GR 2083/ seraphim  60115/emi  1C047 01339M/2C051 01339/ RLS 7713/arabesque  AR 8137
cd: arabesque  Z 6592/emi  586 8332/warner classics  265 0642/music and arts  CD 1173

*10/Schnabel Schubert discography/continued*
**Impromptu in F minor   D935 No 1**

*HMV recording in London Abbey Road Studio No 3
between 8-13 June 1950*
2EA 14761   DB 21382
2EA 14765
45: victor  WHMV 1027
lp: BLP 1030/FALP 295/victor  LHMV 1027/LCT 1019/
electrola  E 80684/toshiba  GR 2083/emi  1C047 01339M/
2C051 01339/RLS 143 5603/arabesque  AR 8145
cd:  arabesque  Z 6572/emi  586 8332/warner
classics  265 0642/music and arts  CD 1173


**Impromptu in A Flat   D935 No 2**

*Concert recording in New York Town Hall on 11 January 1942*
lp:  MJA records  MJA 1966

*HMV recording in London Abbey Road Studio No 3
between 8-13 June 1950*
2EA 14766   DB 21500
2EA 14767
45: 7ER 5042/7ERQ 131/victor  WHMV 1027/EHA 4
lp: BLP 1030/FALP 295/victor  LHMV 1027/LCT 1019/
electrola  E 80684/toshiba  GR 2083/emi  1C047 01339M/
2C051 01339/RLS 143 5603/arabesque  AR 8145
cd:  arabesque  Z 6572/emi  586 8332/warner
classics 265 0642/music and arts  CD 1173

10/Schnabel Schubert discography/continued
**Impromptu in B Flat D935 No 3**

*HMV recording in London Abbey Road Studio No 3
on 12 June 1950*
2EA 14779   DB 21611
2EA 14780
45: victor  WHMV 1027
lp: BLP 1030/FALP 295/victor  LHMV 1027/LCT 1019/
electrola  E 80684/toshiba  GR 2083/emi 1C047 01339M/
2C051 01339/RLS 143 5603/arabesque  AR 8145
cd: arabesque  Z 6572/emi  586 8332/warner
classics  265 0642/music and arts  CD 1173


**Impromptu in F minor D935 No 4**

*HMV recording in London Abbey Road Studio No 3
on 12-13 June 1950*
2EA 14777   DB 21557
2EA 14778
45: 7ER 5042/7ERQ 131/victor  WHMV 1027/EHA 4
lp: BLP 1030/FALP 295/victor  LHMV 1027/LCT 1019/
electrola  E 80684/toshiba  GR 2083/emi  1C047 01339M/
2C051 01339/RLS 143 5603/arabesque  AR 8145
cd: arabesque  Z 6572/emi  586 8332/warner
classics  265 0642/music and arts  CD 1173

10/Schnabel Schubert discography/continued
**6 Moments musicaux D780**

*HMV recording in London Abbey Road Studio No 3
on 2 and 12 November 1937*
2EA 5554    DB 3358/victor  M 684
2EA 5555
2EA 5556    DB 3359/victor  M 684
2EA 5557
2EA 5558    DB 3360/victor  M 684
2EA 5559
lp:  COLH 308/seraphim  1C-6045/emi  RLS 7713/
3C153 01220-01222/EX 29 07883/arabesque  AR 8137
cd:  arabesque  Z 6573/emi  764 2592/warner classics
265 0642/music and arts  CD 1173
*78rpm edition was also published in automatic coupling
with the catalogue numbers  DB 8392-8394*


**Allegretto in C minor D915**

*HMV recording in London Abbey Road Studio No 3
on 25 January 1939*
2EA 7435    DB 3755/DB 9700/DB 8826/DB 21337
lp:  COLH 33/emi  3C153 01220-01222/EX 29 07883/
RLS 7713/arabesque  AR 8137
cd:  emi  586 8332/warner classics  265 0642/
music and arts  CD 1173

10/Schnabel Schubert discography/continued

**Klavierstücke D946: No 1 in E Flat minor**

*Concert recording in New York Town Hall on 18 January 1942*
lp: MJA records  MJA 1966


**Klaviertücke D946: No 2 in E Flat**

*Welte-Mignon piano roll recorded in Freiburg in May 1905*
Roll number  395
cd: tacet  146

*Concert recording in New York Town Hall on 18 January 1942*
lp: MJA records  MJA 1966


**March in E  D606**

*HMV recording in London Abbey Road Studio No 3 on 27 January 1939*
2EA 7447    DB 3760/victor M 888
lp: emi  RLS 143 5603/arabesque  AR 8145
cd: arabesque  Z 6575/emi  764 2592/warner classics  265 0642/music and arts  CD 1173

10/Schnabel Schubert discography/continued
**Scherzi D593: No 1 in B Flat**

*Ampico piano roll recorded in New York City*
*Lane Bryant Building in 1922*
Roll number  62011
lp: klavier  KS 134


**12 Valses nobles  D969**

*Welte-Mignon piano roll recorded in Freiburg in May 1905*
Roll number  385
cd: tacet  146


**3 Marches militaires for piano 4 hands  D733**
with Karl Ulrich Schnabel,  piano

*HMV recording in London Abbey Road Studio No 3*
*on 29 October 1937*
2EA 5539     DB 3527/victor  M 436
2EA 5538
2EA 5537     DB 3528/victor  M 436
lp: electrola  E 80872/toshiba  GR 2136/emi  RLS 7713/ arabesque  AR 8137
cd: music and arts  CD 1173

*10/Schnabel Schubert discography/continued*
**Divertissement a la hongroise for piano 4 hands  D818**
with Karl Ulrich Schnabel, piano

*HMV recording in London Abbey Road Studio No 3
on 28-29 October 1937*
2EA 5516     DB 3529/victor  M 436
2EA 5517
2EA 5518     DB 3530/victor  M 436
2EA 5519
2EA 5520     DB 3531/victor  M 436
2EA 5521
2EA 5522     DB 3532/victor  M 436
2EA 5523
lp: COLH 308/electrola  E 80872/emi  3C153 01220-01222/
RLS 143 5603/arabesque  AR 8145
cd:  music and arts  CD 1173
*78rpm edition was also published in automatic coupling
with the catalogue numbers DB 8812-8815*

*10/Schnabel Schubert discography/continued*
**Grand rondeau in A for piano 4 hands  D951**
with Karl Ulrich Schnabel,  piano

*HMV recording in London Abbey Road Studio No 3
on 28-29 October 1937*
OEA 5526     DA 1644/victor  M 437
OEA 5527
OEA 5528     DA 1645/victor  M 437
OEA 5529
lp: electrola  E 80872/toshiba  GR 2136/
emi  RLS 7713/arabesque  AR 8137
cd:  music and arts  CD 1173


**Allegro in A minor "Lebensstürme" for piano 4 hands  D947**
with Karl Ulrich Schnabel,  piano

*HMV recording in London Abbey Road Studio No 3
on 29 October 1937*
OEA 5530     DA 1646/victor  M 437
OEA 5531
OEA 5532     DA 1647/victor  M 437
OEA 5533
lp:  emi  RLS 143 5603/arabesque  AR 8145
cd:  music and arts  CD 1173

*10/Schnabel Schubert discography/continued*
**Andantino varie (Divertissement a la francais)**
**for piano 4 hands  D823**
with Karl Ulrich Schnabel, piano

*HMV recording in London Abbey Road Studio No 3*
*on 28-29 October 1937*
2EA 5524    DB 3518/victor  M 437
2EA 5525
lp: COLH 308/electrola  E 80872/toshiba  GR 2136/emi
3C153 01220-01222/RLS 143 5603/arabesque  AR 8145
cd: music and arts  CD 1173


**Grands marches  D819:  No 2 in G minor**
with Karl Ulrich Schnabel, piano

*HMV recording in London Abbey Road Studio No 3*
*on 29 October 1937*
2EA 5536    DB 3527/victor  M 436
lp: emi  RLS 7713/arabesque  AR 8137
cd: music and arts  CD 1173

10/Schnabel Schubert discography/continued
**Grands marches D819:  No 3 in B minor**
with Karl Ulrich Schnabel, piano

*HMV recording in London Abbey Road Studio No 3*
*on 29 October 1937*
2EA 5534    victor  M 436
2EA 5535
cd:  music and arts  CD 1173


**Piano Quintet in A  D667  "Die Forelle"**
with members of the Pro Arte String Quartet
and Claude Hobday,  double-bass

*HMV recording in London Abbey Road Studio No 3*
*on 16 November 1935*
2EA 2529    DB 2714/victor  M 312
2EA 2530
2EA 2531    DB 2715/victor  M 312
2EA 2532
2EA 2533    DB 2716/victor  M 312
2EA 2534
2EA 2535    DB 2717/victor  M 312
2EA 2536
2EA 2537    DB 2718/victor  M 312
2EA 2538
lp:  COLH 40/toshiba  GR 2020/emi  2C051 43349/
1C137 53032-53036M/RLS 7713/arabesque  AR 8137
cd:  emi  763 0312/warner classics  265 0642/
music and arts  CD 1173
*78rpm edition was also published in automatic coupling*
*with the catalogue numbers DB 8095-8099*

*10/Schnabel Schubert discography/continued*
**Piano Trio in B Flat D898**
with Joseph Szigeti, violin and Pierre Fournier, cello

*Concert recording in London Westminster Central Hall on 1 October 1947*
lp: discocorp RR 488
cd: music and arts CD 1111


**Schwanengesang D957: Der Doppelgänger** (Still ist die Nacht);
**Die Stadt** (Am fernen Horizonte)
with Therese Behr-Schnabel, contralto

*HMV recording in London Abbey Road Studio No 3 on 16 November 1932*
2B 4511     DB 1833
2B 4512
lp: rococo 5370/emi RLS 143 5603/arabesque AR 8145
cd: dante HPC 135-138/pearl GEMMCDS 9272/ music and arts CD 1173

10/Schnabel Schubert discography/concluded

**Gruppe aus dem Tartarus D583**
(Horch, wie Murmeln des empörten Meeres);
**Der Kreuzzug D932** (Ein Mönch steht in seiner Zell')
with Therese Behr-Schnabel, contralto

*HMV recording in London Abbey Road Studio No 3*
*on 17 November 1932*
2B 4519     DB 1835
2B 4520
lp: rococo 5370/emi RLS 143 5603/arabesque AR 8145
cd: dante HPC 135-138/pearl GEMMCDS 9272/
music and arts CD 1173


**An die Laute D905** (Leiser leiser kleine Laute);
**Der Musensohn D764** (Durch Feld und Wald zu schweifen);
**Erlkönig D328** (Wer reitet so spät durch Nacht und Wind?)
with Therese Behr-Schbabel, contralto

*HMV recording in London Abbey Road Studio No 3*
*on 18 November 1932*
2B 4523     DB 1836
2B 4524
lp: rococo 5370/emi RLS 766 (der musensohn)/RLS 143 5603/
1C135 78111-78118M (der musensohn)/arabesque AR 8145
cd: emi 566 1502/dante HPC 135-138/pearl GEMMCDS 9270/
music and arts CD 1173

## 11/A REMARKABLE SCHUBERT EVENING
*Christian Blackshaw played the last three Sonatas at the Wigmore Hall in London on 19 November 2014*

As with Mozart's last three Symphonies and their incredible richness of expression, I have always felt that performing these final Sonatas as a single entity, within the framework of one evening, is almost too much of a good thing, certainly too much to digest in the short span of a couple of hours. It might even encourage us, I often reflected, to take the works for granted.

Christian Blackshaw offered a solution to the problem by spacing the three Sonatas with a full-length concert interval between each one. This enhanced the sense of an epic journey on the part of both performer and listener, added to which our concentration was further aided by having the Wigmore Hall almost totally plunged into darkness, save for a few exit lights. The only previous pianist I can recall having done this was Sviatoslav Richter in some of his final London recitals.

All of the above would of course be quite irrelevant if the performances on offer were not of sufficient artistic stature. And also, to invoke the name of Richter when talking about Schubert playing is to place enormous pressure and responsibility on any pianist who approaches such core repertoire.

*11/A remarkable Schubert evening/continued*

Gavin Plumley's astute programme note drew attention to what must have been the intense pressure on the composer himself, who, in the twelve months left to him after he had served as a pall-bearer at Beethoven's funeral, to come up with something in sonata form which might be worthy of comparison with the German master. After all, of all the various complete and incomplete piano sonatas which Schubert had himself produced over the years of his short life, only three had up to this time actually appeared in print (these were D845, D850 and D894).

Heavenly length in sonata or symphonic movements can of course be a questionable thing if the executant cannot sufficiently sustain a sense of forward propulsion (among conductors, Wilhelm Furtwängler and Reginald Goodall could do this with mastery). I do not for one moment hesitate to place Christian Blackshaw in this category: each sonata, and within it each individual movement, was given generous breathing space within the over-all framework: even concluding *allegro* movements, with their sense of immense release after the foregoing introspection, were integrated in masterly fashion.

## 11/A remarkable Schubert evening/concluded

When the three works are played like this as a triptych, the centrepiece D959 seems to me to stand as the ultimate masterpiece out of the three, plumbing depths on its course but yet concluding in serene optimism. The second movement of that work, misleadingly described as *Andantino,* had threatened to abandon tonality and verged on collapse, before finally returning to comforting sanity. After such a poignant realisation of this, Blackshaw went on to stress that we are here never far away from the world of song: the concluding *Allegretto* of the sonata bearing more than a strong resemblance, in its thematic material, to Schubert's *Das Lied im Grünen.*

There is probably no pianist active today who would wish to be compared to Richter, but the shade of Christian Blackshaw's mentor Clifford Curzon certainly rose up at points during this remarkable recital (the few recorded examples which we have of Curzon playing Schubert show a very similar poise between introspection and momentum).

Despite concerted efforts by certain audience members to mar the evening with their coughing and their mobile devices, it is to be hoped that the engineers can overcome this sufficiently in order to publish these important Schubert interpretations on Wigmore Hall's own CD label. On the other hand, is it not perhaps obscene even to wish to preserve such a life-changing experience in mechanical form and for endless repetition?

John Hunt

## 12/INDEX OF PIANISTS
*Numbers refer to the pages on which a pianist's name occurs*

**Adrian Aeschbacher** (1912-2002)
091      096

**Geza Anda** (1921-1976)
091

**Leif Ove Andsnes** (born 1970)
083      087      091

**Martha Argerich** (born 1941)
120

**Claudio Arrau** (1903-1991)
077      085      087      089
091      096      099      100
102

*12/Index of pianists/continued*
**Paul Badura-Skoda** (born 1927)

| 059 | 062 | 066 | 067 |
| 068 | 069 | 071 | 072 |
| 073 | 075 | 076 | 078 |
| 080 | 085 | 087 | 091 |
| 095 | 100 | 101 | 102 |
| 113 | 114 | 117 | 118 |
| 120 | | | |

**Daniel Barenboim** (born 1942)

| 063 | 069 | 072 | 078 |
| 081 | 085 | 087 | 089 |
| 091 | 097 | 098 | 120 |

**Christian Blackshaw** (born 1949)
173-175

*12/Index of pianists/continued*

**Paolo Bordoni** (born 1953)

| 103 | 104 | 109 | 110 |
| 111 | 112 | | |

**Alfred Brendel** (born 1931)

| 064 | 069 | 074 | 081 |
| 085 | 087 | 091 | 095 |
| 099 | 100 | 103 | 110 |
| 111 | | | |

**Benjamin Britten** (1913-1976)

| 114 | 115 | 117 | 118 |
| 145 | | | |

**Caroline Clemmow**

| 113 | 114 | 115 | 117 |
| 118 | 120 | 122 | |

**Imogen Cooper** (born 1949)

| 078 | 080 | 081 | 083 |
| 085 | 087 | 089 | 091 |
| 099 | 114 | | |

**Clifford Curzon** (1907-1982)

| 083 | 091 | 095 | 097 |
| 098 | 175 | | |

*12/Index of pianists/continued*

**Joerg Demus** (born 1928)
| | | | |
|---|---|---|---|
| 096 | 097 | 098 | 099 |
| 113 | 114 | 117 | 118 |
| 120 | | | |

**Youri Egorov** (1954-1988)
087

**Michael Endres** (born 1961)
| | | | |
|---|---|---|---|
| 061 | 066 | 067 | 069 |
| 070 | 074 | 081 | 085 |
| 087 | 091 | 104 | 107 |
| 109 | | | |

**Eduard Erdmann** (1896-1958)
| | | | |
|---|---|---|---|
| 085 | 087 | 089 | 091 |

**Christoph Eschenbach** (born 1940)
| | | | |
|---|---|---|---|
| 089 | 091 | 114 | 115 |
| 116 | 117 | 118 | 119 |
| 120 | 121 | | |

*12/Index of pianists/continued*

**Edwin Fischer** (1886-1960)
095  097  098

**Leon Fleisher** (born 1928)
091  111

**Justus Frantz** (born 1944)
114  115  116  117
118  119  120  121

**David Fray** (born 1981)
085  103  118  119

**Nelson Freire** (born 1944)
120

**Paolo Giacometti** (born 1970)
078

**Emil Gilels** (1916-1985)
078  083

**Robert Goldsand** (1911-1991)
097  098

*12/Index of pianists/continued*

**Anthony Goldstone** (1945-2017)

| 091 | 095 | 096 | 098 |
| --- | --- | --- | --- |
| 100 | 113 | 114 | 115 |
| 117 | 118 | 120 | 122 |

**Friedrich Gulda** (1930-2000)

| 096 | 097 |
| --- | --- |

**Ingrid Haebler** (born 1929)

| 063 | 068 | 069 | 072 |
| --- | --- | --- | --- |
| 074 | 077 | 081 | 085 |
| 087 | 089 | 091 | 096 |
| 097 | 098 | 113 | 117 |
| 118 | | | |

**Clara Haskil** (1895-1960)

| 007 | 081 | 091 |
| --- | --- | --- |

**Myra Hess** (1890-1965)

077

*12/Index of pianists/continued*

**Ludwig Hoffmann** (1925-1999)
| | | |
|---|---|---|
| 113 | 117 | 118 |

**Vladimir Horowitz** (1903-1989)
091

**Eileen Joyce** (1908-1991)
100

**Cyprien Katsaris** (born 1951)
091

**Wilhelm Kempff** (1895-1991)
| | | | |
|---|---|---|---|
| 061 | 062 | 066 | 067 |
| 068 | 069 | 070 | 071 |
| 073 | 076 | 080 | 081 |
| 085 | 087 | 089 | 091 |
| 095 | 099 | 100 | 104 |

**Sebastian Knauer** (born 1971)
| | | | |
|---|---|---|---|
| 087 | 097 | 098 | 100 |
| 103 | | | |

**Alfons Kontarsky** (1932-2010)
115

**Alois Kontarsky** (born 1931)
115

*12/Index of pianists/continued*

**Lili Kraus**  (1903-1986)

| | | | |
|---|---|---|---|
| 077 | 078 | 081 | 089 |
| 091 | 095 | 098 | 102 |
| 109 | 110 | 111 | 112 |
| 113 | 115 | | |

**Elisabeth Leonskaya**  (born 1945)

| | | | |
|---|---|---|---|
| 065 | 078 | 081 | 083 |
| 087 | 089 | 091 | 100 |

**Paul Lewis**  (born 1972)

| | | | |
|---|---|---|---|
| 065 | 078 | 080 | 083 |
| 087 | 089 | 091 | 099 |
| 114 | 115 | 118 | 119 |
| 120 | | | |

**Nikolai Lugansky**  (born 1972)

| | |
|---|---|
| 087 | 103 |

*12/Index of pianists/continued*

**Radu Lupu**  (born 1945)

| | | | |
|---|---|---|---|
| 064 | 070 | 077 | 081 |
| 085 | 087 | 096 | 103 |
| 118 | | | |

**Homero de Magalhaes**  (1924-1997)

| | |
|---|---|
| 113 | 115 |

**Alexander Melnikov**  (born 1973)

| | | |
|---|---|---|
| 115 | 118 | 120 |

**Arturo Benedetti Michelangeli**  (1925-1995)

069

**Eldar Nebolsin**  (born 1974)

| | | |
|---|---|---|
| 069 | 077 | 095 |

**Elly Ney**  (1892-1968)

095

**Gerhard Oppitz**  (born 1953)

| | | | |
|---|---|---|---|
| 061 | 080 | 081 | 085 |
| 087 | 091 | 095 | 096 |
| 097 | 098 | 099 | 100 |
| 101 | 102 | 103 | 104 |

12/Index of pianists/continued

**Steven Osborne**  (born 1971)
115         118         119         120

**Murray Perahia**  (born 1947)
118

**Francesco Piemontesi**  (born 1983)
089

**Maria Joao Pires**  (born 1944)
081         091         097         098
099

**Maurizio Pollini**  (born 1942)
087         089         091

*12/Index of pianists/continued*

**Sviatoslav Richter** (1915-1997)

| | | | |
|---|---|---|---|
| 007 | 011 | 065 | 071 |
| 073 | 074 | 076 | 077 |
| 078 | 080 | 081 | 083 |
| 085 | 087 | 092 | 095 |
| 099 | 100 | 102 | 104 |
| 109 | 114 | 115 | 117 |
| 118 | 125-151 | 173 | |

**Hans Richter-Haaser** (1912-1980)

| | |
|---|---|
| 078 | 087 |

**Jacques Rouvier** (born 1947)

| | |
|---|---|
| 118 | 119 |

**Andras Schiff** (born 1953)

| | | | |
|---|---|---|---|
| 060 | 081 | 089 | 100 |

**Artur Schnabel** (1882-1951)

| | | | |
|---|---|---|---|
| 011 | 077 | 083 | 089 |
| 092 | 096 | 097 | 098 |
| 100 | 102 | 103 | 114 |
| 115 | 117 | 119 | 120 |
| 153-171 | | | |

12/Index of pianists/continued

**Karl Ulrich Schnabel** (1909-2001)
114   115   117   119
120   165-169

**Rudolf Serkin** (1903-1991)
080   089   092   096

**Andreas Staier** (born 1955)
115   118   120

**Martino Tirimo** (born 1942)
059   062   073

**Mitsuko Uchida** (born 1948)
063   089   092

**Arcadi Volodos** (born 1972)
066   085

*12/Index of pianists/concluded*

**Friedrich Wührer** (1900-1975)

| | | | |
|---|---|---|---|
| 060 | 062 | 069 | 072 |
| 074 | 076 | 078 | 080 |
| 081 | 083 | 085 | 087 |
| 089 | 092 | | |

**Christian Zacharias** (born 1950)

| | | |
|---|---|---|
| 064 | 081 | 087 |

**Dieter Zechlin** (1926-2012)

| | | | |
|---|---|---|---|
| 060 | 062 | 066 | 067 |
| 068 | 069 | 071 | 072 |
| 074 | 076 | 078 | 081 |
| 085 | 087 | 089 | 092 |
| 096 | | | |

## 13/POSTSCRIPT

### SCHUBERT CDs FOR THE DESERT ISLAND
*A personal recommendation*


**18 Piano Sonatas**
Dieter Zechlin
Berlin Classics  018 4482BC  (8 CDs)

**17 Piano Sonatas & Complete Solo Dance Music**
Michael Endres
Capriccio  C 7125  (10 CDs)

**8 Piano Sonatas & Miscellanrous Piano Works**
Sviatoslav Richter
Profil Medien  PH 17005  (10 CDs)

**Piano Sonatas  D845 and D960**
Maria Joao Pires
Deutsche Grammophon  477 8107  (1 CD)

**Works for Piano 4-hands**
Christoph Eschenbach and Justus Frantz
EMI  569 7642 and 569 7702  (4 CDs)

**Wanderer Fantasy,  Hüttenbrenner Variations and other solo pieces**
Wilhelm Kempff
Deutsche Grammophon  453 2892  (1CD)

**Impromptus  D899 and D935**
Daniel Barenboim
Deutsche Grammophon  415 9492  (1CD)

## Books published by Travis & Emery Music Bookshop:

Anon.: Hymnarium Sarisburiense, cum Rubricis et Notis Musicis.
Anon.: Säcularfeier des Geburtstages von Ludwig van Beethoven
Agricola, Johann Friedrich from Tosi: Anleitung zur Singkunst.
Allen, Percy: The Stage Life of Mrs. Stirling: With ... C19$^{th}$ Theatre
Bach, C.P.E.: edited W. Emery: Nekrolog or Obituary Notice of J.S. Bach.
Bateson, Naomi Judith: Alcock of Salisbury
Bathe, William: A Briefe Introduction to the Skill of Song
Berlioz, Hector: Autobiography of Hector Berlioz, (2 vols.)
Buckley, Robert John: Sir Edward Elgar
Burney, Charles: The Present State of Music in France and Italy
Burney, Charles: The Present State of Music in Germany, The Netherlands ...
Burney, Charles: Account of an Infant Musician
Burney, Charles: An Account of the Musical Performances ... Handel
Burney, Karl: Nachricht von Georg Friedrich Handel's Lebensumstanden.
Burns, Robert: The Caledonian Musical Museum .. Best Scotch Songs. (1810)
Cobbett, W.W.: Cobbett's Cyclopedic Survey of Chamber Music. (2 vols.)
Corrette, Michel: Le Maitre de Clavecin
Cox, John Edmund: Musical Recollections of the Last Half Century. (2 vols.)
Crimp, Bryan: Dear Mr. Rosenthal ... Dear Mr. Gaisberg ...
Crimp, Bryan: Solo: The Biography of Solomon
Crotch, William: Substance of Several Courses of Lectures on Music
d'Indy, Vincent: Beethoven: Biographie Critique
d'Indy, Vincent: Beethoven: A Critical Biography
d'Indy, Vincent: Cesar Franck (in English)
d'Indy, Vincent: César Franck (in French)
Dianna, B.A.: Benjamin Britten's Holy Theatre
Dolge, Alfred: Pianos and Their Makers. A Comprehensive History
Fischhof, Joseph: Versuch einer Geschichte des Clavierbaues. (Faksimile 1853).
Fuller-Maitland, J.A.: The Music of Parry and Stanford
Geminiani, Francesco: The Art of Playing the Violin.
Häuser: Musikalisches Lexikon. 2 vols in one.
Hawkins, John: A General History of the Science & Practice of Music (5 vols.)
Holmes, Edward: A Ramble among the Musicians of Germany
Hopkins, Antony: The Concertgoer's Companion - Bach to Haydn.
Hopkins, Antony: The Concertgoer's Companion – Holst to Webern.
Hopkins, Antony: Music All Around Me
Hopkins, Antony: Sounds of Music / Sounds of the Orchestra
Hopkins, Antony: The Nine Symphonies of Beethoven
Hopkins, Antony: Understanding Music

**Books published by Travis & Emery Music Bookshop:**

Hopkins, Edward & Rimboult, Edward: The Organ. Its History & Construction.
Hunt, John: - see separate list of discographies at the end of these titles
Iliffe, Frederick: The Forty-Eight Preludes and Fugues of John Sebastian Bach
Isaacs, Lewis: Hänsel and Gretel. A Guide to Humperdinck's Opera.
Isaacs, Lewis: Königskinder (Royal Children). Guide to Humperdinck's Opera.
Kastner: Manuel Général de Musique Militaire
Kenney, Charles Lamb: A Memoir of Michael William Balfe
Klein, Hermann: Thirty years of musical Life in London, 1870-1900
Lacassagne, M. l'Abbé Joseph : Traité Général des élémens du Chant
Lascelles (née Catley), Anne: The Life of Miss Anne Catley.
McCormack, John: John McCormack: His Own Life Story.
Mainwaring, John: Memoirs of the Life of the Late George Frederic Handel
Malcolm, Alexander: A Treaty of Music: Speculative, Practical and Historical
Manshardt, Thomas: Aspects of Cortot
Marx, Adolph Bernhard: Die Kunst des Gesanges, Theoretisch-Practisch
May, Florence: The Life of Brahms
May, Florence: The Girlhood Of Clara Schumann: Clara Wieck And Her Time.
Mellers, Wilfrid: Angels of the Night: Popular Female Singers of Our Time
Mellers, Wilfrid: Bach and the Dance of God
Mellers, Wilfrid: Beethoven and the Voice of God
Mellers, Wilfrid: Caliban Reborn - Renewal in Twentieth Century Music
Mellers, Wilfrid: Darker Shade of Pale, A Backdrop to Bob Dylan
Mellers, Wilfrid: François Couperin and the French Classical Tradition
Mellers, Wilfrid: Harmonious Meeting
Mellers, Wilfrid: Le Jardin Retrouvé, The Music of Frederic Mompou
Mellers, Wilfrid: Music and Society, England and the European Tradition
Mellers, Wilfrid: Music in a New Found Land: … … American Music
Mellers, Wilfrid: Romanticism and the Twentieth Century (from 1800)
Mellers, Wilfrid: The Masks of Orpheus: …… the Story of European Music.
Mellers, Wilfrid: The Sonata Principle (from c. 1750)
Mellers, Wilfrid: Vaughan Williams and the Vision of Albion
Newmarch, Rosa: Henry J. Wood
Newmarch, Rosa: Jean Sibelius
Newmarch, Rosa: Mary Wakefield, a Memoir
Newmarch, Rosa: The Concert-Goer's Library
Newmarch, Rosa: The Music of Czechoslovakia
Newmarch, Rosa: The Russian Opera.
Nicholas, Jeremy: Godowsky, the Pianists' Pianist
Niecks, Frederick: The Life oc Chopin. (2 vols.)

## Books published by Travis & Emery Music Bookshop:

Panchianio, Cattuffio: Rutzvanscad Il Giovine
Pearce, Charles: Sims Reeves, Fifty Years of Music in England.
Pepusch, John Christopher: A Treatise on Harmony ...
Pettitt, Stephen: Philharmonia Orchestra: A Record of Achievement, 1948-1985
Pettitt, Stephen (ed. Hunt): Philharmonia Orchestra: Discography 1945-1987
Playford, John: An Introduction to the Skill of Musick.
Porte, John: Sir Charles Villiers Stanford.
Quantz, Johann: Versuch einer Anweisung die Flöte traversiere zu spielen.
Rameau, Jean-Philippe: Code de Musique Pratique, ou Methodes.
Rameau, Jean-Philippe: Erreurs sur La Musique dans l'Encyclopédie
Rastall, Richard: The Notation of Western Music.
Rimbault, Edward: The Pianoforte, Its Origins, Progress, and Construction.
Rousseau, Jean Jacques: Dictionnaire de Musique
Rubinstein, Anton : Guide to the proper use of the Pianoforte Pedals.
Sainsbury, John S.: Dictionary of Musicians. (1825). (2 vols.)
Schumann, Clara & Brahms, Johannes: Letters 1853-1896. (2 vols.)
Scott-Sutherland: Arnold Bax
Serré de Rieux, Jean de : Les dons des Enfans de Latone
Simpson, Christopher: A Compendium of Practical Musick in Five Parts
Smyth, Ethel: Impressions That Remained. (2 vols.)
Spohr, Louis: Autobiography
Spohr, Louis: Grand Violin School
Tans'ur, William: A New Musical Grammar; or The Harmonical Spectator
Terry, Charles Sanford: Bach's Chorals – Parts 1, 2 and 3.
Terry, Charles Sanford: John Christian Bach
Terry, Charles Sanford: J.S. Bach's Original Hymn-Tunes - Congregational Use.
Terry, Charles Sanford: Four-Part Chorals of J.S. Bach. (German & English)
Terry, Charles Sanford: Joh. Seb. Bach, Cantata Texts, Sacred and Secular.
Terry, Charles Sanford: The Origins of the Family of Bach Musicians.
Tosi, Pierfrancesco: Opinioni de' Cantori Antichi, e Moderni
Tosi, Pierfrancesco: Observations on the Florid Song.
Tovey, Donald Francis: A Musician Talks, The Integrity of Music
Tovey, Donald Francis: A Musician Talks, Musical Textures
Tovey, Donald Francis: A Companion to "The Art of the Fugue" J.S. Bach
Tovey, Donald Francis: A Companion to Beethoven's Pianoforte Sonatas
Tovey, Donald Francis: Beethoven
Tovey, Donald Francis: Essays in Musical Analysis. (6 vols.).
Tovey, Donald Francis: The integrity of music
Tovey, Donald Francis: Musical Textures

**Books published by Travis & Emery Music Bookshop:**

Tovey, Donald Francis: Some English Symphonists
Tovey, Donald Francis: The Main Stream of Music.
Van der Straeten, Edmund: History of the Violoncello, The Viol da Gamba ...
Van der Straeten, Edmund: History of the Violin, Its Ancestors... (2 vols.)
Walther, J. G. [Waltern]: Musicalisches Lexikon [Musikalisches Lexicon]
Wagner, Richard: Beethoven (Leipzig 1870)
Wagner, Richard: Lebens-Bericht (Leipzig 1884)
Wagner, Richard: The Musaic of the Future (Translated by E. Dannreuther).
Wyndham, Henry Saxe: The Annals of Covent Garden Theatre. (2 vols.)
Zwirn, Gerald: Stranded Stories From The Operas

**Music published by Travis & Emery Music Bookshop:**

Bach, Johann Sebastian: Sacred Songs for SCTB, arranged by Franz Wullner.
Bax, Arnold: Symphony #5, Arranged for Piano Four Hands by Walter Emery
Beranger, Pierre Jean de: Musique Des Chansons de Beranger: Airs Notes ...
Bizet, Georges: Djamileh. Vocal Score.
Donizetti, Gaetano: Betly. Dramma Giocoso in Due Atti. Vocal Score.
Frescobaldi, Girolamo: D'Arie Musicali per Cantarsi. Primo & Secondo Libro.
Handel, Purcell, Boyce, Greene ... Calliope or English Harmony: Volume First.
Hopkins, Antony: Sonatine
Purcell, Henry et al: Harmonia Sacra ... The First Book, (1726)
Purcell, Henry et al: Harmonia Sacra ... Book II (1726)
Sullivan, Arthur Seymour: Ivanhoe. Vocal score.
Sullivan, Arthur Seymour: The Rose of Persia. Vocal Score.
Weckerlin, Jean-Baptiste: Chansons Populaires du Pays de France

**Other Books, not on Music:**

Anon: A Collection of Testimonies Concerning Several Ministers of the Gospel
          Amongst People called Quakers, Deceased. [Facsimile of 1760 edn.].
Sandeman-Allen, Arthur: Bee-keeping with Twenty hives.

Available from: Travis & Emery at 17 Cecil Court, London, UK.
(+44) (0) 20 7 240 2129. email on sales@travis-and-emery.com .

## Discographies by John Hunt.

3 Italian Conductors and 7 Viennese Sopranos: 10 Discographies: Arturo Toscanini, Guido Cantelli, Carlo Maria Giulini, Elisabeth Schwarzkopf, Irmgard Seefried, Elisabeth Gruemmer, Sena Jurinac, Hilde Gueden, Lisa Della Casa, Rita Streich.

A Gallic Trio: 3 Discographies: Charles Muench, Paul Paray, Pierre Monteux.

A Notable Quartet: 4 Discographies: Gundula Janowitz, Christa Ludwig, Nicolai Gedda, Dietrich Fischer-Dieskau.

American Classics: The Discographies of Leonard Bernstein & Eugene Ormand

Antal Dorati 1906-1988: Discography and Concert Register.

Austro-Hungarian Pianists, Discographies of Lili Kraus, Friedrich Gulda, Ingrid Haebler

Back From The Shadows: 4 Discographies: Willem Mengelberg, Dimitri Mitropoulos, Hermann Abendroth, Eduard Van Beinum.

Carlo Maria Giulini: Discography and Concert Register.

Columbia 33CX Label Discography.

Concert Hall Discography: Concert Hall Society and Concert Hall Record Club

Conductors On The Yellow Label: 8 Discographies: Fritz Lehmann, Ferdinand Leitner, Ferenc Fricsay, Eugen Jochum, Leopold Ludwig, Artur Rother, Franz Konwitschny, Igor Markevitch.

Dirigenten der DDR: Conductors of the German Democratic Republic

Fremd bin ich eingezogen - a critical discography of the piano music of Franz Schubert

From Adam to Webern: the Recordings of von Karajan.

Frosh: Discography of the Richard Strauss Opera Die Frau ohne Schatten

Giants of the Keyboard: 6 Discographies: Wilhelm Kempff, Walter Gieseking, Edwin Fischer, Clara Haskil, Wilhelm Backhaus, Artur Schnabel.

Gramophone Stalwarts: 3 Separate Discographies: Bruno Walter, Erich Leinsdorf, Georg Solti.

Great Violinists: 3 Discographies: David Oistrakh, Wolfgang Schneiderhan, Arthur Grumiaux.

Hans Knappertsbusch: Kna: Concert Register and Discography of Hans Knappertsbusch, 1888-1965. Second Edition.

Her Master's Voice: Concert Register and Discography of Dame Elisabeth Schwarzkopf [Third Edition].

Hungarians in Exile: 3 Discographies: Fritz Reiner, Antal Dorati, George Szell.

Leopold Stokowski (1882-1977): Discography and Concert Register

Leopold Stokowski: Discography and Concert Listing.

Leopold Stokowski: Second Edition of the Discography.

Makers of the Philharmonia: 11 Discographies Alceo Galliera, Walter Susskind, Paul Kletzki, Nicolai Malko, Issay Dobrowen, Lovro Von Matacic, Efrem Kurtz, Otto Ackermann, Anatole Fistoulari, George Weldon, Robert Irving.

Metropolitan Sopranos: 4 Discographies: Rosa Ponselle, Eleanor Steber, Zinka Milanov, Leontyne Price.

Mezzo and Contraltos: 5 Discographies: Janet Baker, Margarete Klose, Kathleen Ferrier, Giulietta Simionato, Elisabeth Hoengen.

Mid-Century Conductors and More Viennese Singers: 10 Discographies: Karl Boehm, Victor De Sabata, Hans Knappertsbusch, Tullio Serafin, Clemens Krauss, Anton Dermota, Leonie Rysanek, Eberhard Waechter, Maria Reining, Erich Kunz.

More 20th Century Conductors: 7 Discographies: Eugen Jochum, Ferenc Fricsay, Carl Schuricht, Felix Weingartner, Josef Krips, Otto Klemperer, Erich Kleiber.
More Giants of the Keyboard: 5 Discographies: Claudio Arrau, Gyorgy Cziffra, Vladimir Horowitz, Dinu Lipatti, Artur Rubinstein.
More Musical Knights: 4 Discographies: Hamilton Harty, Charles Mackerras, Simon Rattle, John Pritchard.
Musical Knights: 6 Discographies: Henry Wood, Thomas Beecham, Adrian Boult, John Barbirolli, Reginald Goodall, Malcolm Sargent.
Philharmonic Autocrat 1: Discography of: Herbert Von Karajan [3rd Edition]
Philharmonic Autocrat 2: Concert Register of Herbert Von Karajan 2nd. Ed.
Philharmonic Autocrat: Discography of Herbert von Karajan (1908-1989). 4th Ed..
Philips Minigroove: Second Extended Version of the European Discography.
Pianists For The Connoisseur: 6 Discographies: Arturo Benedetti Michelangeli, Alfred Cortot, Alexis Weissenberg, Clifford Curzon, Solomon, Elly Ney.
Record Pioneers: Richard Strauss, Hans Pfitzner, Oskar Fried, Oswald Kabasta, Karl Muck, Franz Von Hoesslin, Karl Elmendorff.
Sächsische Staatskapelle Dresden: Complete Discography.
Singers of the Third Reich: 5 Discographies: Helge Roswaenge, Tiana Lemnitz, Franz Voelker, Maria Mueller, Max Lorenz.
Singers on the Yellow Label: 7 Discographies: Maria Stader, Elfriede Troetschel, Annelies Kupper, Wolfgang Windgassen, Ernst Haefliger, Josef Greindl, Kim Borg
Six Wagnerian Sopranos: 6 Discographies: Frieda Leider, Kirsten Flagstad, Astrid Varnay, Martha Moedl, Birgit Nilsson, Gwyneth Jones.
Staatskapelle Berlin. The shellac era 1916-1962.
Sviatoslav Richter: Pianist of the Century: Discography.
Teachers and Pupils: 7 Discographies: Elisabeth Schwarzkopf, Maria Ivoguen, Maria Cebotari, Meta Seinemeyer, Ljuba Welitsch, Rita Streich, Erna Berger
Tenors in a Lyric Tradition: 3 Discographies: Peter Anders, Walther Ludwig, Fritz Wunderlich.
The Art of the Diva: 3 Discographies: Claudia Muzio, Maria Callas, Magda Olivero.
The Furtwaengler Sound Sixth Edition: Discography and Concert Listing.
The Furtwängler Sound. Discography of Wilhelm Furtwängler. Seventh Edition.
The Great Dictators: 3 Discographies: Evgeny Mravinsky, Artur Rodzinski, Sergiu Celibidache.
The Lyric Baritone: 5 Discographies: Hans Reinmar, Gerhard Huesch, Josef Metternich, Hermann Uhde, Eberhard Waechter.
The Post-War German Tradition: 5 Discographies: Rudolf Kempe, Joseph Keilberth, Wolfgang Sawallisch, Rafael Kubelik, Andre Cluytens.
Wagner Im Festspielhaus: Discography of the Bayreuth Festival.
Wiener Philharmoniker 1 - Vienna Philharmonic and Vienna State Opera Orchestras: Discography Part 1 1905-1954.
Wiener Philharmoniker 2 - Vienna Philharmonic and Vienna State Opera Orchestras: Discography Part 2 1954-1989.
Wiener Staatsoper: 348 complete relays

Available from: Travis & Emery at 17 Cecil Court, London, UK.
(+44) (0) 20 7 240 2129. email on sales@travis-and-emery.com .

www.ingramcontent.com/pod-product-compliance
Lightning Source LLC
Chambersburg PA
CBHW070824250426
43671CB00036B/2068